Windows on Music

Windows on Music
Learning with *Practica Musica*

Jeffrey Evans

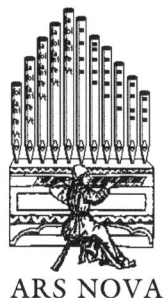

ARS NOVA

Printed in the United States of America

Third Edition
revision 7/96

1 2 3 4 5 6 7 8 9 10 — 98 97 96

ISBN 0-929444-03-5

Library of Congress Catalogue Card Number: 88-71355

Cover graphics: Steven Brown, Santa Barbara Artworks
Monophonic music examples created with Ars Nova's *Songworks.*

Table of Contents

Appendices

Preface

This text is meant to accompany the computer program *Practica Musica*. Together, the text and *Practica Musica* provide both an explication of the basic theory and practice of tonal music and practical experience with musical sounds and their notation. Because the software is interactive it can also function as a tutor in correcting the student's work and reinforcing the knowledge gained in the book.

The subject matter covered in the text is that of an introductory "music theory" course, though the "supplementary" sections of some chapters will at times go beyond the essentials of an introduction. Similarly, the software has something for both beginners and more advanced students: the higher levels of play in each activity can be challenging to anyone, while the correction capabilities and friendly patience of the computer should help even the shyest novice.

The software largely takes the place of written exercises, and it keeps progress records that can be printed out and submitted to a teacher just as a written exercise would be. But I have also provided separately some written exercises with the goal of giving the student experience in putting music on paper. Certain tasks, after all, are best done by hand — for reasons both practical and aesthetic.

I want to thank the critical readers, Dr. John Carbon of Franklin and Marshall College, Dr. Kenneth Rumery of Northern Arizona University, and Scott Zeidel of the University of California at Santa Barbara. In that category also belongs my wife Patricia; her expertise as a performing musician has been as much of a help as her ability with language. I would also like to thank Lynn Maners of the University of California at Los Angeles, who read this text from the viewpoint of a non-musician, and the many people who have contributed ideas to Practica Musica itself.

Introduction

The object of our study is the musical language developed in Europe over the course of the last 1000 years, particularly the "tonal" music that is associated with such composers as Bach, Mozart and Beethoven and which also forms the basis of modern popular music.

What we want to learn first about this language of sound is its notation—how to read it and how to write down what we hear or imagine in a way that can be easily understood by others.

Along the way to musical literacy we'll gain some insights into how tonal music came to be, and we'll acquire familiarity with its basic materials: the *beat*, the *measure, major* and *minor scales*, and *triads*. We'll study the way that the basic materials of music are built into melody and harmony, and describe principles that can help you to write music of your own. If you take an interest in traditional music of other cultures, or in western jazz or avant-garde music, you will find that this knowledge retains its usefulness.

Using this book with *Practica Musica*

 Most chapters will contain activity boxes marked with the Practica Musica icon, shown at left. The activity boxes contain suggestions for the effective use of Practica Musica in support of the material discussed in the chapter. In general you will do best by going through the Practica Musica activities roughly in menu order, but skipping the higher levels of each until you have absorbed some of what each one has to offer. You'll also find that in addition to the organized activities, Practica Musica can serve as a valuable learning tool by identifying chords you play in the "practice harmony" mode or simply by displaying notes on the staff as they are depressed ("practice melody") or by labeling the keys with the appropriate note-names (the "staff keyboard" in the Keyboards menu) or by providing such esoteric services as an illustration of the theoretical pitch difference between "enharmonic" notes (see p. 26).

Practica Musica can also provide an acoustic illustration of many of the musical examples in these pages, so that you can both see the examples and hear them. Examples that are available for listening are marked with a small Practica Musica icon, and are kept in the Melodies folder. You can hear the example by going to the Melody Writing/ Listening activity and using the "Open melody" command to locate the example that interests you. You can even make temporary changes in the example and listen to them, if you would like to experiment.

For instance, the example depicted in Figure 10 of Chapter 11 is the theme from the last movement of Brahms' 1st Symphony. You'll find it, complete with chords, in a file called "Chapter 11, Figure 10."

I. SCALES AND THE KEYBOARD

The two basic elements of music are *pitch* and *rhythm*. "Pitch" refers to the "highness" or "lowness" of a note. "Rhythm" refers to the pattern in time made by a series of notes. Standard music notation provides a simple way to represent both pitch and rhythm.

To understand the notation of pitch you first will need to understand the concept of the *scale*, which is a group of pitches used as the "raw material" of a composition. Actually a scale is not so much a set of specific pitches as it is a *pattern* of large and small musical steps, known as *halfsteps* and *wholesteps*. The best way to explain these is to let you hear them.

1

Activity

Start Practica Musica and then select the "Staff Keyboard" from the Student Options menu. The staff keyboard shows you the letter names of the white keys: A through G.

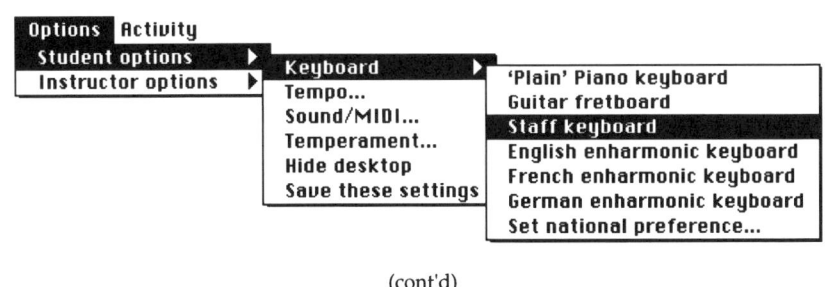

(cont'd)

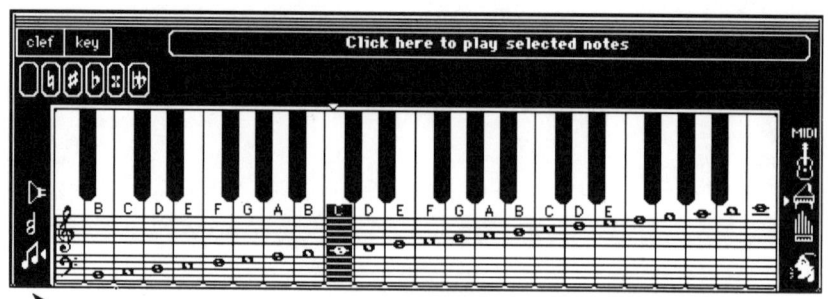

Click the mouse on the "melody" icon at the lower left of the screen keyboard and then slide the mouse up the piano keys as if you were playing the piano with one finger. Play only the white keys for now.

Can you tell that E and F sound closer together than D and E? How about the difference between B-C and C-D? Listen carefully several times until you can tell the difference. The musical distance from E to F and from B to C is a *halfstep*; all the other white keys are separated by *wholesteps*.

Now try sliding on the white keys from C upward to the next C. You'll hear the notes C, D, E, F, G, A, B, C. This pattern of wholesteps (W) , and halfsteps (H) is called the *major scale*: WWHWWWH. Play it both ascending and descending until you can imagine the sound of each note before hearing it.

Solmization

A good way to remember the major scale pattern is to practice singing it with the *solmization* syllables *do, re, mi, fa, sol, la, si,* pronounced "dough, ray, me, fah, soul, lah, sea." The pattern of steps made by these syllables corresponds to the sound of the white keys of the piano starting with "C," as on your Practica Musica keyboard:

$$\begin{array}{ccccccc}
C & D & E & F & G & A & B & C \\
\text{do} & \text{re} & \text{mi} & \text{fa} & \text{sol} & \text{la} & \text{si} & \text{do}
\end{array}$$

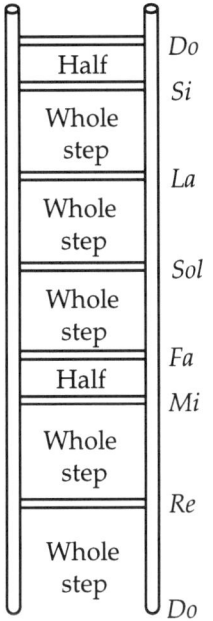

Figure 1: Major scale

In the "C major scale," (the major scale that begins on C), *do* is C, *re* is D, *mi* is E, and so on. So the halfsteps E-F and B-C use the syllables *mi-fa* and *si-do*. Since the word "scale" comes from the Latin word for "ladder" you could visualize the scale steps as rungs on a ladder, as in Figure 1.

Moveable *do* and fixed *do*

In this book the syllable *do* will always represent the first note of a major scale, a system that is called the *moveable do* system. So if we start a major scale on E then E would be called *do*. In France and Italy the *fixed do* system is traditional (see Practica Musica's 'French' enharmonic keyboard); in that system the note C is always called *do*, even if it is not the first note of the scale being used. Each system has its advantages, but you'll find that the moveable *do* system makes it easier for you to sing the major scale starting on any pitch.

Octaves and the concept of *pitch class*

If you listened to the scale formed by the white keys of the keyboard you may have heard that after seven notes the scale seems to start over again with the same pattern. That's because the eighth note, which we say is an *octave* away from where we started (*octo*=eight) sounds very much like the C that we began with, only higher. It sounds that way because it has exactly twice the frequency (see the appendix on the physics of music) of the first C, and since we hear it as essentially the same pitch we give it the same letter name. In fact, all our scales just go as far as the octave of their starting note and then they repeat, so you could say that *a scale is a pattern of steps for filling in the space of an octave.*

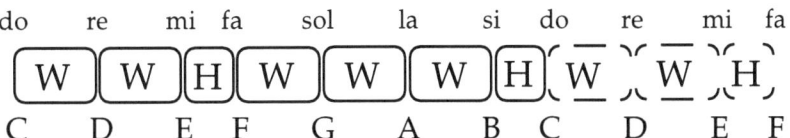

Figure 2: The scale pattern repeats at the octave

2

Activity

Click the "harmony" button on your Practica Musica keyboard (the button just above the melody button) and then click on all the C's you can find on the keyboard. Click the "play selected notes" button to hear them all together. Now add any note that has a different letter name— such as B. Can you hear that all the C's sound like basically the same pitch, but the B seems to be something altogether different? But if you turn off those notes (click again on the keyboard notes) and then try playing all the B's you'll again find that all B's sound very similar to each other. They differ only in *octave*.

Musicians say that notes that are octaves of each other, such as the C's or the B's, have the same *pitch class*. The keyboard's white keys really include only seven pitch classes, and all the others are octaves of those seven. This should make your task of learning music seem much easier: a large piano may have 52 white keys, but they are just the same seven pitches repeated in different octaves.

The design of the keyboard

Early keyboards — those made about the same time that solmization was invented — had only white keys, since they were designed to play just the notes of what we now call the C major scale.

But if your keyboard has only white keys, what happens if you want to play the major scale starting on some note other than C? This would be called *transposing* the major scale pattern. Try it yourself: remember that the steps for the major scale are W W H W W W H — can you play that pattern starting on F? *Remember that among the white keys there are halfsteps only between E and F and between B and C.*

If you have only the white keys to work with you'll run into trouble on the step between your third and fourth notes (A and B) — it will make a wholestep instead of the required halfstep. But you can fix your keyboard by adding another key whose pitch is midway between A and B. Then the major scale on F can be played as follows:

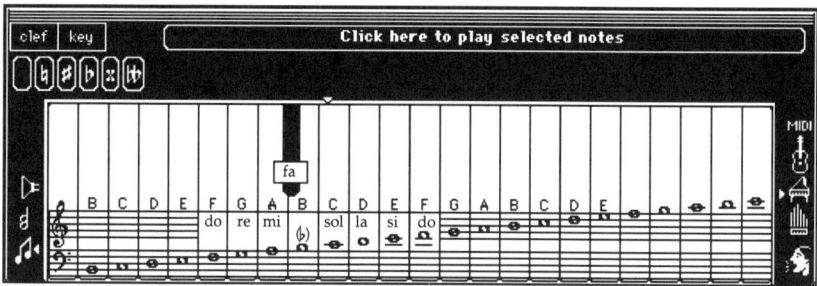

Figure 3: Adding black keys to the keyboard

Since the fourth note of the scale was going to be named B we will say that this lowered version is still a kind of B: it is "B flat," a B played a halfstep lower than its unaltered form. In fact, this was the first black key to be added to the keyboard, and that's how the flat symbol ♭ came to resemble a small "b": early composers wrote the higher form of B (the one on the white key) with square edges (♮) and the lower form with rounded edges (♭). They felt that the higher form was "harder" (B *durum*) while the lower one played on the black key was "softer" (B *molle*). You may recognize the "hard B" symbol as the precursor of the modern *natural* sign (♮) which is now used to indicate a note played in its unaltered form, on the white keys. Another descendent of the former "hard B" sign is the *sharp* (♯) which is used for notes that are *raised* a half step.

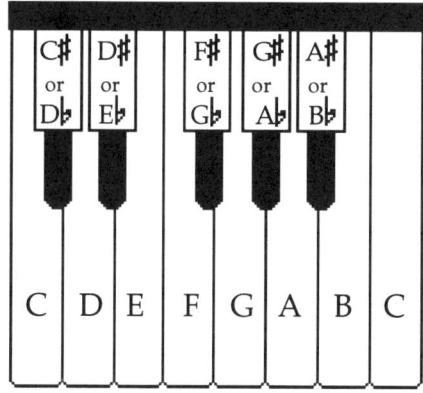

Figure 4: The role of the black keys

Eventually, black keys were added to fill in every wholestep on the keyboard; they allow you to play major or minor scales or melodies beginning on any note you choose. The black keys ended up grouped in threes and twos because on the original plain white keyboard E to F and B to C are halfsteps— you don't need a black key in those places.

The names of the black keys vary according to how you're using them: the one between F and G, for example, may be called "F sharp,"an F raised one halfstep, or it may be called "G flat," a G lowered one halfstep, just as the "B flat" we started with could also be called "A sharp" given the right circumstances. For example, if we start a major scale on D its third note will be some kind of F (D, E, F — the letters are always in order and none is repeated or left out). But E to F is only a halfstep and we need a wholestep here to make a major scale, so we raise the F one half-step and call it F sharp:

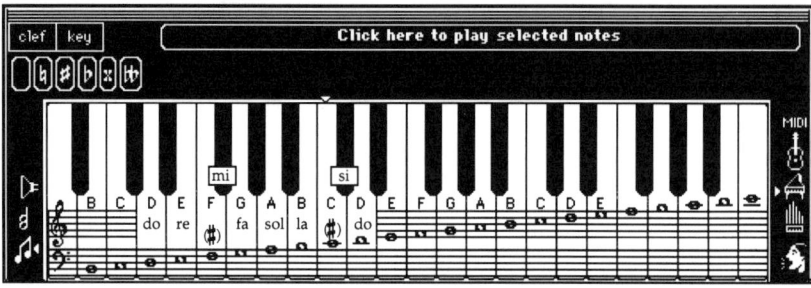

Figure 5: Naming the black keys in D major

We'll later see that the white keys can also have different names: F can be called E sharp, E can be F flat, and so on.

3

Activity

Practica Musica can teach you how to play a major scale beginning on any note. Just choose Scales from the Activities menu and then select Level 1 from the Scales menu. You'll be asked to play major scales on the keyboard, and Practica Musica will guide you when you need help.

The natural minor scale

The major scale is only one of the possible ways to arrange whole steps and half steps to fill in an octave. Another important scale is the *natural minor* scale, which is the pattern of steps you hear if you play the white (natural) keys starting on or A, or *la*. The natural minor scale starting on A consists of the notes A, B, C, D, E, F, G, A, and its steps are arranged as in Figure 6: W H W W H W W.

The relative minor and relative major

The major scale starting on C and the minor scale starting on A each use the same notes: C, D, E, F, G, A, and B. We say that A minor is the *relative minor* of C major and that C major is the *relative major* of A minor. In the C major scale A is *La*: the sixth note. Every major scale, no matter what note it starts on, has a relative minor that begins with its *La*, or sixth note. The relative minor uses exactly the same notes as its relative major, but just starting from a different place. For example, D major uses the notes D, E, F#, G, A, B, and C#. The sixth note of the D major scale is B, and so we can say that the relative minor of D major starts on B: B, C#, D, E, F#, G, A, B.

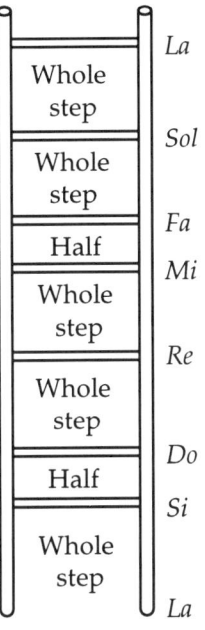

Figure 6: Natural minor scale

4

Activity

Using Practica Musica with the Melody button on, try sliding the mouse up the white keys beginning at A. You'll hear the notes of "A natural minor," which are A, B, C, D, E, F, G, A (easy to remember). Listen carefully to the pattern of wholesteps and halfsteps that defines the minor scale and compare it to the sound of the major scale that begins on C. Does the minor scale seem to have a "darker" mood to it? Many people have thought so in the past.

Now do as much as you can in Level 2 of the Scales activity. It is like Level 1 except that it deals with the natural minor scale.

The *tonic, dominant,* and *subdominant*

You may have noticed that the first note of a scale can give the impression of being more important than the others. This first note, called the *tonic,* is the one that is generally used to end a melody — an ending on any other note sounds incomplete. Each scale also has a *dominant* note that is almost as important as the tonic and which is the fifth scale step upward from it, and there is even a *subdominant* which is, as you might guess, the fifth scale step *downward* from the tonic. In solmization the names for these are *do, sol,* and *fa,* also known as I, V, and IV. In the below illustration the keys are marked to show the tonic (T), dominant (D), and subdominant (S) degrees of the C major scale, which are the notes C , G, and F.

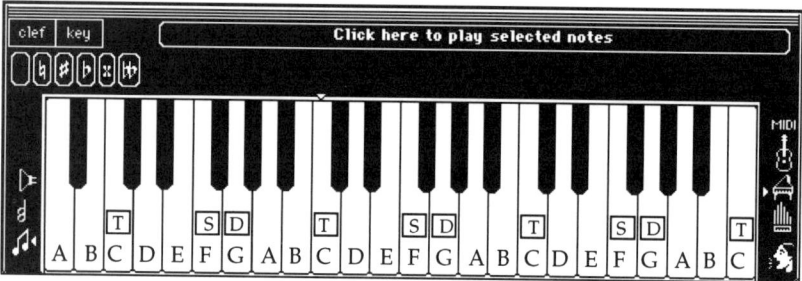

Figure 7: Tonic, Dominant, and Subdominant degrees of C major

The reason these three are so important is partly due to history and partly to acoustics. The dominant seems to have a particularly close acoustic relationship to the tonic, which can make it seem to be the "main note" of a melody, next to the tonic itself. And the tonic is the same distance above the subdominant as the dominant is above the tonic.

Tonic, subdominant, and dominant in the minor scale

Now that you've seen the minor scale pattern, what would be the dominant of the minor scale that begins on A? As in the major scale, it would be the fifth scale note from the tonic, counting upward. You can count A, B, C, D, E: E is the dominant. The subdominant is once again the note that is the fifth scale note *downward* from the tonic. In A minor that would be D (D is also the note one scale step below the dominant, so you may prefer to think of it that way). Note that we are counting *scale notes* — not piano keys. When counting scale notes we skip the keys that aren't in the scale.

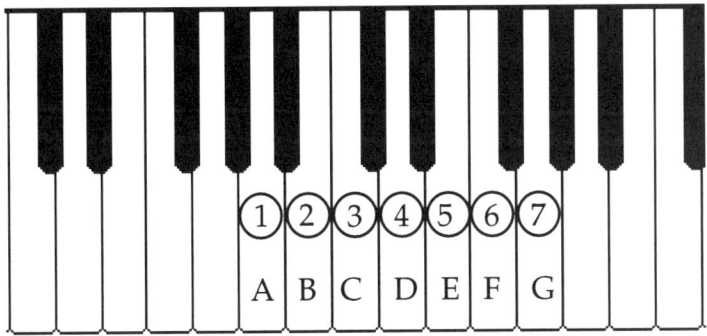

Figure 8: Counting degrees of the A natural minor scale

The importance of scales

Why is it useful to know scales? Because almost any popular melody can be shown to consist of no more than the seven notes of a single major or minor scale. Look, for example, at this familiar tune:

do   do   re   si   do   re   mi   mi   fa   mi   re   do   re   do   si   do
My Coun-try, 'tis of thee, sweet land of li-   ber- ty, of thee I sing...

The melody so far consists of nothing more than five notes of the major scale: *si, do, re, mi,* and *fa*. Once you know how to sing a major scale it is an easy thing to sing this song, or almost any other. Very few well-known tunes use more than seven pitch classes; many use less.

This will also provide your first clue to successful composition or improvisation: *popular tunes tend to use only the notes of a single scale and they usually end on the first note of that scale.*

It would be good practice for you to sing this melody to yourself using the solmization syllables instead of words. Try singing it in the *key* of C major (that is, using the C major scale). Play the notes B, C, D, E, F, and call them *si, do, re, mi,* and *fa.* (we're starting with *si* instead of *do* because this song uses the *si* just below *do* instead of the *si* above it). Then sing:

> *do do re si, do re*
> *mi mi fa mi, re do*
> *re do si do . . .*

The keyboard below is marked to show you where to find the syllables for the first part of *My Country, 'Tis of Thee.*

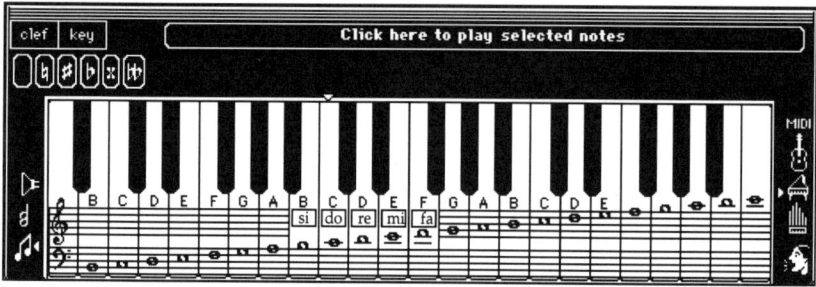

Figure 9: Finding the notes of *My Country, 'tis of Thee*

The advantage of solmization is that once you know the sound of the syllables; once you know that *mi-fa* and *si-do* are halfsteps and the others are wholesteps, then you can easily learn any song that uses a major or minor scale (which is most of them).

5

Activity

The first part of *My Country, 'tis of Thee* (also known as *God save the King*) is in the Practica Musica melody library for Level 1.

Practica Musica will play the start of this tune for you and it will also write it on the screen if you click the correct notes on the keyboard. Choose Pitch Dictation from the Activities menu, and then choose Library Melodies, Level 1 from the Pitch Dictation menu. From the list that appears, select *My Country.*

(cont'd)

Then select the Staff Keyboard from the Keyboard Options menu, if you haven't already, and use it as a guide while you click the mouse on these keys.

The first C is provided, so begin with the sec ᴐnd one:

(C) C D B C D   E E F E D C   D C B C

Notice that the tune has appeared in *staff notation,* which is a much better way of writing down music than just using letters alone. In the next chapter we'll learn how the staff system works, but for now just click the Play button and listen as the melody is played. You can also use this as a guide to sing along with the solmization syllables.

SUPPLEMENTARY TOPICS, CHAPTER I

The other degrees of the scale

Just as the words *tonic, subdominant,* and *dominant* refer to the first, fourth, and fifth notes or *degrees* of a scale, there are also names for the other degrees.

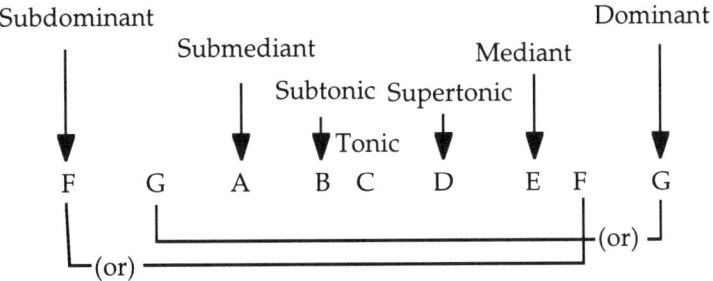

Figure 10: Names for the degrees of the scale, using C major as an example. (The notes separated by a halfstep are drawn closer together than the others.)

The *mediant*, the third degree or note of the scale, gets its name from being halfway between the tonic and the dominant — in a sense it *mediates* between them. Similarly the *submediant* is three steps down, mediating between the tonic and the subdominant. Finally there's the *supertonic*, which is the first note up from the tonic, and the *subtonic*, the first one down. In the major scale we can also refer to the subtonic as the *leading tone*, because it is just a halfstep away from the tonic and seems to "lead" back to it. Of course, since we've established the fact of *octave equivalence* — the fact that notes with the same name are interchangeable — you'll see that any F may be considered the subdominant in C major, and any G may be called the dominant.

The scale degree names work the same way for a minor scale, except that the natural minor has no "leading tone:"

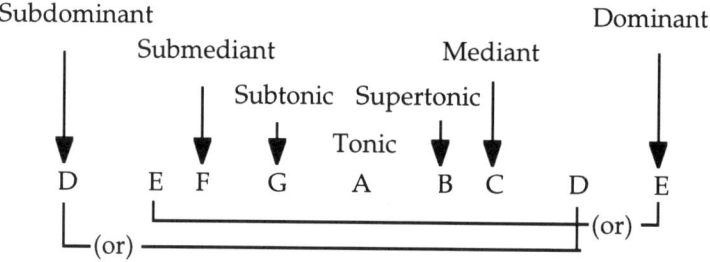

Figure 11: Degrees of the natural minor scale, using A minor as an example.

Summary, Chapter I

1. *Pitch* refers to the "highness" or "lowness" of a note.

2. A *halfstep* is the smallest musical step on the keyboard; a *wholestep* is equal to two halfsteps. From E to F is a halfstep; from C to D is a wholestep.

3. An *octave* is the distance between, for example, low C and middle C on the Practica Musica keyboard. It represents a doubling of the frequency of a note. Notes that are octaves of each other have the same *pitch class*. There are many keys on a piano but only twelve pitch classes. The white keys include only seven pitch classes.

4. A *scale* is a certain pattern of wholesteps and halfsteps that divides up the space in an octave. We form music from the notes of scales.

5. The white keys beginning on C show the pattern of the *major scale*: W W H W W W H. The white keys starting on A show the *natural minor* pattern: W H W W H W W.

6. The solmization syllables *do, re, mi, fa, sol, la, si* help you to memorize the pattern of steps that forms the major scale. The steps *mi-fa* and *si-do* are always half steps; the others are whole steps. The same solmization syllables present the natural minor scale if you start on *la* instead of on *do*.

7. Each major scale has a *relative minor* scale that uses the same notes but starts three scale steps lower. Conversely, each minor scale has a *relative major* scale that starts three scale steps higher.

8. Most popular melodies use just the seven notes of a single scale, and they usually end on the tonic, or starting note, of the scale.

9. The black keys on the keyboard fill in the halfstep between each of the white key pairs that is separated by a wholestep. They can have different names: the same black key may be called G flat (G lowered one halfstep) or F sharp (F raised one halfstep). The white keys can also have different names: F, for example, can be called E#.

10. The first note or *degree* of a scale is its *tonic;* the fifth note is its *dominant;* the fourth note is its *subdominant.*

Supplementary Topics:

11. The seven degrees of a major or minor scale are called the *tonic, supertonic, mediant, subdominant, dominant, submediant, and leading tone* (or *subtonic*).

II. NOTATION OF PITCH

The staff

If you already know the rhythm of a song you can remember its melody by just writing down the name of each of its notes, as we did in Chapter I for *My Country, 'Tis of Thee*. This works well enough for simple pieces, but fortunately there is a better way, one that can show both the rhythm and the pitch and which is also quicker to read. *Staff notation* is based on the idea of writing note symbols on a group of horizontal lines

The wholenote

and spaces that represent the scale. The line or space used identifies the pitch and the shape of the notes tells the rhythm. For now we'll need only one note-shape, the *wholenote*.

The staff used today has five lines (originally it was just one and for a while it was four), and notes can be drawn either on a line or on the space between two lines. The lines and spaces refer to the notes of the

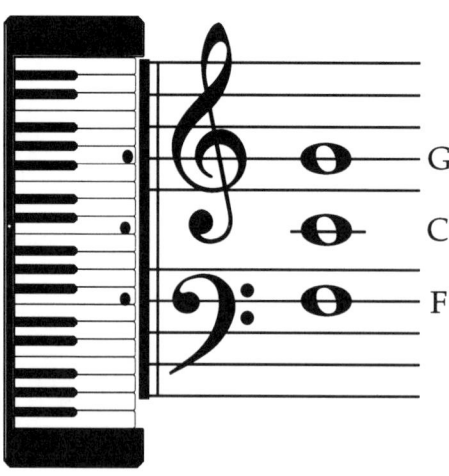

Figure 2: The grand staff

natural scale (the white keys of the keyboard), and a *clef* sign is placed at the beginning of the staff to indicate which lines are which.

The most common *clefs* are the G-clef, or *treble clef,* and the F-clef, or *bass clef. Clef* comes from the French word for "key," and you can see that it does act as a key to understanding the staff notation: the G-clef circles the line representing the G above "middle C" (the C that is midway between the two clefs) and the two dots of the F-clef mark the line taken by the F below middle C. Often the treble and bass staffs are used together in a combination known as the *grand staff,* as in Figure 2.

Notice that the lines and spaces of the staff correspond to the white keys of the piano! If you move to the next line or space you move to the next white key and the next letter name, the sound of which can be either a whole step or a half step higher. For example, from the second line of a treble clef to its second space is the wholestep G - A. But the distance from the third line to the third space is the halfstep B - C:

G-A (wholestep)   B-C (halfstep)

Figure 3: Not all staff steps are the same

Reading staff notation

Students of music often use mnemonic devices to remember which notes are which in the bass and treble clefs. For example, "FACE" and "All Cows Eat Grass" remind you of the notes for the spaces in the treble and bass clefs. "Every Good Bird Does Fly" can be used for the lines of the treble clef. If you forget these devices just remember that the treble clef circles G and the bass clef points to F, and that every line and space represents a letter in ascending alphabetical order from A through G.

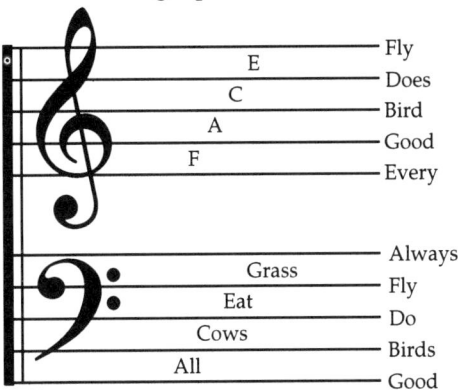

Figure 4: Ways to remember the notes of the treble and bass clefs

6

Activity

Select Pitch Reading from Practica Musica's Activities menu, and then choose Level 1 from the Pitch Reading menu. In Pitch Reading you'll be asked to play a series of notes written in staff notation, without worrying about rhythm. You can either play them with the mouse on the *Practica Musica* screen keyboard or you can use an electric instrument equipped with MIDI (any MIDI instrument can be used — a keyboard or even a guitar).

For Level 1 you'll be dealing with just the naturals (the white keys). You may find it helpful to use the Staff Keyboard as we did earlier (it's available from the Options menu). Work carefully, even though this is a timed exercise — you lose more points by a wrong note than you gain by moving quickly. On the other hand, once you're confident enough to move quickly your score will increase with your speed.

When you find the right piano key the corresponding note will sound and will appear highlighted in the staff. When you hit the wrong key you'll hear an unmusical sound and Practica Musica will wait for you to locate the correct key. If you are not sure which piano key is correct, just click the mouse on the staff note, like this:

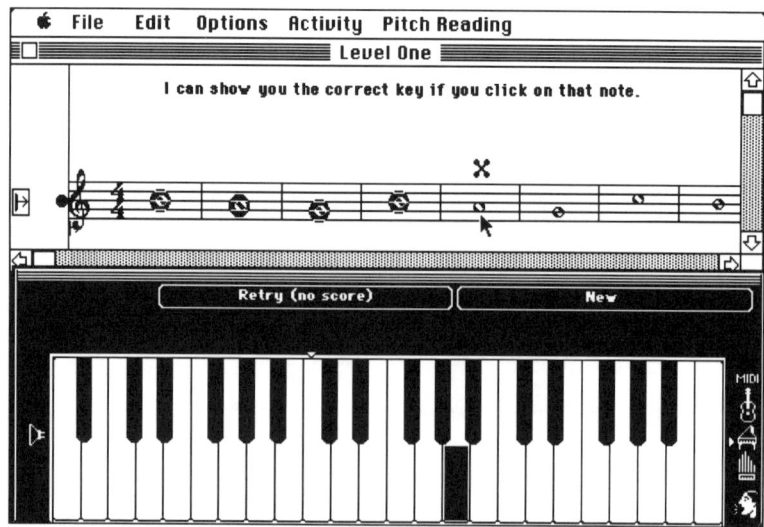

Writing music by hand

Even though computers can do an excellent job of printing music there will be many times when you will need to be able to copy it out by hand. This skill is particularly useful if you happen to think of a nice musical idea at a time when all you have to work with is a paper and pencil. There's also a certain pleasure to be found in writing music by hand, which you can discover as you gain skill. Finally, writing musical exercises by hand is a good way to help you learn the material.

Remember that everyone has an individual style of handwriting, and yet the symbols need to be easily recognizable by others. Your first efforts at writing should be made with great care to follow a model; later you can go more quickly and you'll find that your own style will develop naturally. We can begin with the treble clef and bass clef.

Figure 5: Forming the treble and bass clefs

Here are a few examples of clefs drawn by famous composers, just to inspire you:

Bach

Mozart

Beethoven

Figure 6: Handwriting samples

Now that you've got the clefs, try putting down some notes. So far, all we've seen is the wholenote. Keeping in mind that the wholenote is not round but oval, try to write out the C scale both ascending and descending, as follows (staff paper is provided in the back of this book).

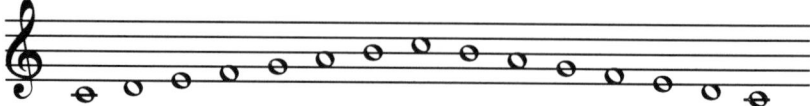

Figure 7: Ascending and descending C major scale, in wholenotes

Ledger lines

What is the purpose of the short line through the C that begins this scale? It is a *ledger line* (sometimes spelled *leger*), which is an extension of the staff system. We needed to put in a ledger line because neither the treble clef nor the bass clef goes as far as middle C. To write a note that is higher or lower than the limits of the staff you add more lines, but you make them short — just a little wider than the note. Try writing out the following C major scales:

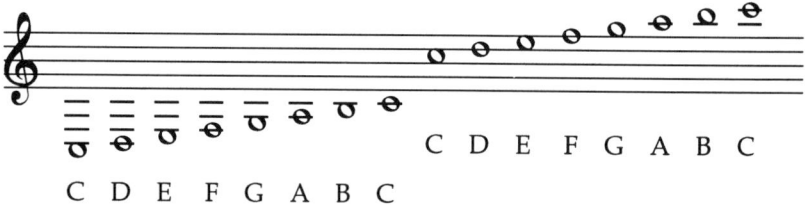

Figure 8: Using ledger lines

Ledger lines provide a good way to extend the reach of the staff without making it harder to read. Several centuries ago some musicians tried drawing staffs with as many as ten lines, but you can imagine how difficult to read that must have been! The five-line staff has remained the standard, probably because it is hard to read any more lines without losing track of which one is which.

Sharps, flats, and naturals

A sharp (♯) added to a note raises it a halfstep; a flat (♭) means to lower it by a halfstep.   In most cases a sharp or flat will put you on a black key, but not always. Notice, for example, that a "C♭" will be played on the same key as B (since B is a halfstep lower than C). The natural sign (♮) reminds you that a note is to be played in its natural form, on the white key that bears its name.

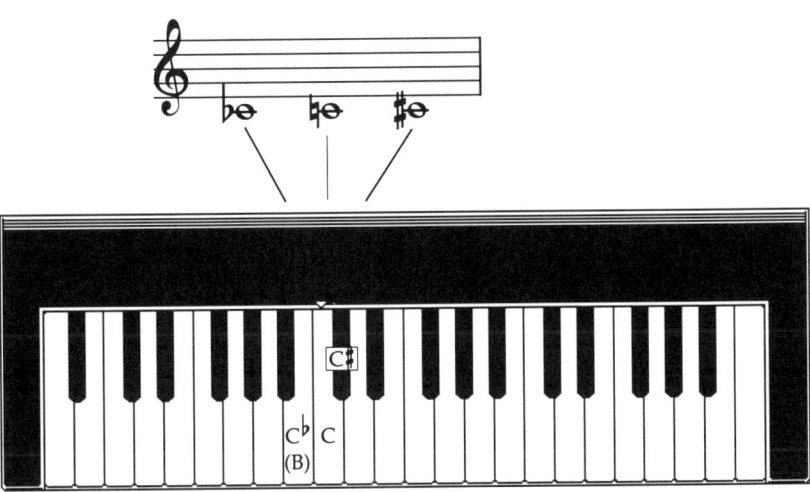

Figure 9: Playing sharps and flats

Activity

7

If you have already "graduated" from Level 1 of Pitch Reading this would be a good time to try Level 2. In Level 2 you'll begin to see sharps or flats appear before some of the notes. Again you can click on the note to see which key is used to play it, and again you'll be scored for accuracy and time. This is a litle harder than Level 1, naturally, and it may take you many sessions before you can build up enough points to graduate from Level 2. If you quit Practica Musica it will save your "game in progress" so that you can return to it where you left off.

Key signatures

If you write a piece using the notes of the F major scale and ending on F the piece may be said to be in the *key* of F major.

We've already seen that if you want to write a tune using notes of the F major scale you will need to use the flat form of the B. That means that in the key of F the B flat will be needed throughout the piece. Rather than write the flat every time a B appears it is easier to just indicate it once at the beginning of each staff. This is the reason for the *key signature*, the collection of sharps or flats you will often see at the start of each line of music in a printed score. The *key signature* for F major is a single flat sign placed on the B-line of the staff. A musician reading the signature will remember to lower all the B's to B flat:

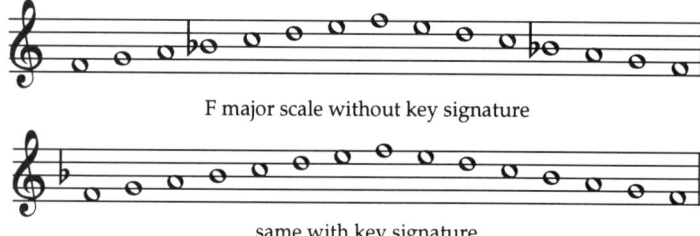

F major scale without key signature

same with key signature

Figure 10: Using a key signature

Similarly, the A major scale requires F#, G#, and C#, so pieces written for that scale use a key signature of three sharps:

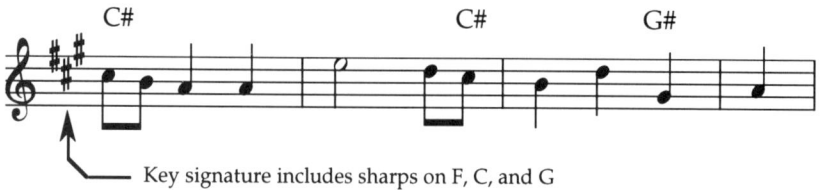

Key signature includes sharps on F, C, and G

Figure 11: Melody using "A major" key signature

A key signature is printed at the beginning of each line and stays in effect until canceled by another one. Whenever you write a clef you should follow it by the key signature.

The sharps or flats in a key signature are always displayed in a standard arrangement to make them easier to recognize. Here are all fourteen signatures and their keys, as drawn in the treble and bass clefs:

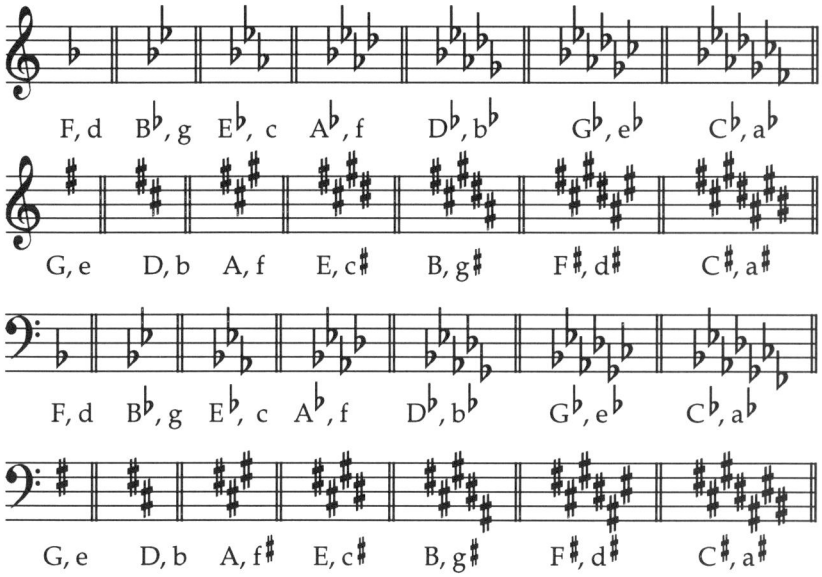

Figure 12: The key signatures. Upper case = major key; lower case = minor

Notice that flats and sharps are never mixed in a key signature — the signature is always just one or the other. Also, the flats or sharps are always added in the same order: the first flat is always Bb and the first sharp is always F#; the second sharp is always C#, and so on. This helps you to quickly identify the notes — if a key has only two sharps in its signature they will always be F# and C#: you don't need to look at their placement in the staff. For example, the below illustration shows the order in which sharps are added to a key signature:

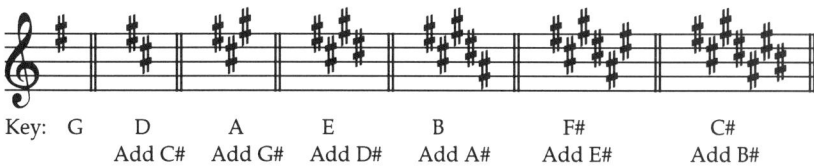

Figure 13: Building key signatures

The *circle of fifths* is often used to show how flats or sharps are added in a key signature; it is built on the principle that when the tonic rises a fifth the key signature gets a new sharp that is a fifth higher than the previous sharp; when the tonic drops a fifth the key signature gets a new flat that is a fifth lower than the previous flat.

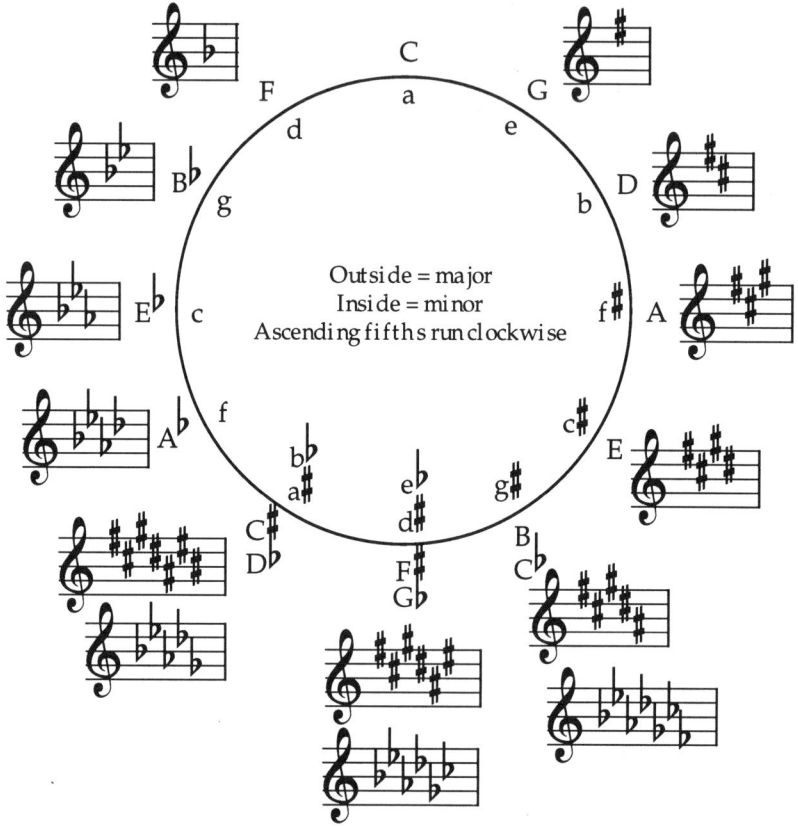

Figure 14: The circle of fifths

Usually students just memorize the signatures: one sharp means G major or E minor; two means D major or B minor, etc. But there is a shortcut to identifying a key from its signature. Notice that the last sharp in a key signature is always the seventh degree of the major scale for that key, or the second degree of the corresponding relative minor scale:

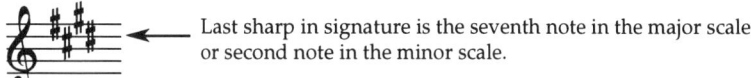

Last sharp in signature is the seventh note in the major scale or second note in the minor scale.

Figure 15: Identifying a sharp signature

In Figure 15 the last sharp is D#, so we know that the scale being used is either E major or C# minor.

Similarly, the last flat in a flat signature can help you identify a flat key:

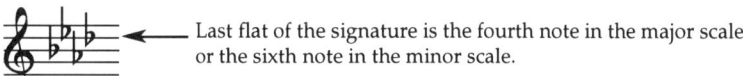

Last flat of the signature is the fourth note in the major scale or the sixth note in the minor scale.

Figure 16: Identifying a flat key signature

Of course, both of these methods require that you know whether the piece is major or minor! For now you can generally just check the last note of the piece, which is almost always the tonic. So a piece with a two-sharp key signature that ends on B is probably in B minor rather than D major. Once you learn chords there will be no doubt of the key, but that comes later.

The convenience of key signatures

Now that we understand the function of key signatures let's examine several more scales, just to make a point.

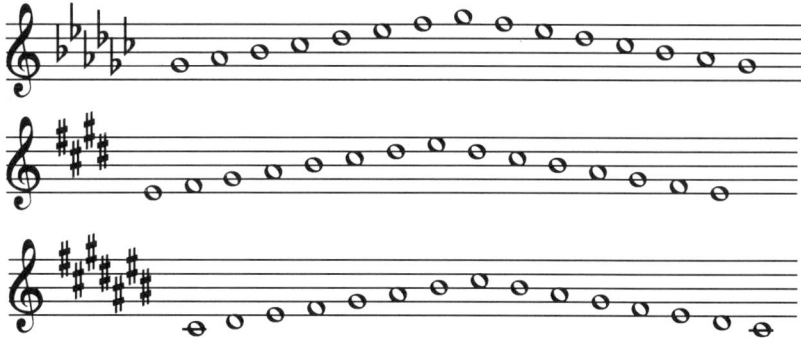

Figure 17: Several scales

Though the scales may involve many sharps or flats, the pattern of notes on the staff looks the same for all of them. The key signature takes care of all necessary sharps or flats. *If we're writing a melody that uses only the notes of a single major or natural minor scale we'll never need to add any sharps or flats, since they are provided by the key signature.*

8

Activity

Choose the "Custom" level of Pitch Reading. Leave the default settings untouched for now. When the first exercise appears you can use the "Key" box in the keyboard tools to pick particular key signatures to work with. Try signatures with as many as 5 flats or sharps. You'll be surprised how quickly you get used to them. Keys with 6 or 7 sharps/flats are uncommon, but playing in such keys will further increase your skill.

Accidentals

If you see a sharp or a flat written in a piece it means that the changed note is not part of the prevailing major scale or natural minor scale, since the key signature supplies all the scale notes for major and natural minor. Sharps and flats used to alter scale notes are known as *accidentals*. They last only until the end of the measure (a measure is the space between two measure lines); if the altered note is used again in the next measure then a new accidental must be written.

The term is a little confusing — accidentals are not "accidental" at all, but very deliberate! As mentioned earlier, the sharp, ♯ , raises a note one halfstep, and the flat, ♭ , lowers it the same amount. You may also see a *double-sharp*, usually written as 𝄪, and a *double-flat*, ♭♭, which raise or lower the note by two half-steps.

The natural, ♮ , can be used to cancel any of the other accidentals, or to cancel (until the barline) a flat or sharp in the key signature.

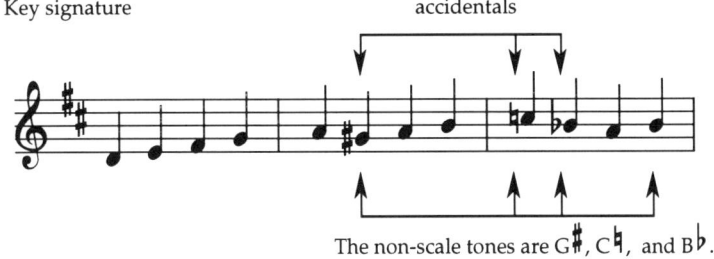

Figure 18: Using accidentals

Notice that in the last measure of Figure 18 the second Bb doesn't need an accidental. The flat is still in effect from earlier in the measure.

Since the key signature supplies all the sharps or flats that are part of the major or natural minor scale, you will need to write accidentals only when you depart from one of those scales in some way. This will happen sometimes when you switch to another scale in the course of a piece (known as *modulating*, or *changing key*) or when you just add something extra for a special effect. The sight of an accidental in a measure always means that a note has been used that was not included in the key signature.

Precautionary accidentals

Since accidentals last only until the next measure line you have to write them again if you want to repeat the same accidental in the next measure. Nonetheless, composers often remind the reader that an accidental is no longer in effect by marking the note explicitly with a *precautionary accidental* in the next measure, like this:

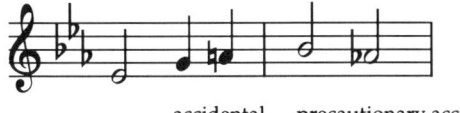

accidental   precautionary accidental

Figure 19: A precautionary accidental

In this example the A would have reverted to Ab anyway, but the flat was written in as a reminder.

9
Activity

You should attempt Level 4 of Pitch Reading, although it may seem difficult at first. In Level 4 you will encounter all sorts of key signatures and the melody will often include accidentals. Once you have graduated from all four of the Pitch Reading levels then you certainly will be able to say that you know how to read pitches in the treble and bass clefs.

Enharmonic equivalents

Enharmonic equivalents are notes that have different names but are played by the same piano key. For example, the black key between F and G can be called either F# or Gb, so F# and Gb are enharmonic equivalents. The same is true of Fb and E, both of which are played on the E key of the piano. Enharmonic equivalents sound the same on a piano, since they are played by the same key, but they have different musical meanings. We'll discover later, for instance, that F# could be part of a D chord, but Gb could not. Also, enharmonic equivalents can actually have slightly different pitches on some instruments. F# and Gb are in theory not exactly the same pitch, though for convenience we tune the piano so that one key can play both of them [see the appendix on *temperament*].

10
Activity

Select the "Enharmonic keyboard" from the Options menu of Practica Musica, and then click on the "melody button" at the lower left of the screen keyboard, as we did in Activity 1. Now go to the Tuning menu and select "Extended meantone" (this won't work if you're using MIDI — you must be using Macintosh sound). Extended meantone is a way of tuning the Practica Musica keyboard so that you can hear the theoretical difference between enharmonic equivalents. Now click on the note C and slide the mouse down to B#. These notes would be played on the same key on an ordinary piano, but on this special keyboard you can hear the difference between them. The same is true of the black keys, which are divided into their enharmonic sharps and flats. Can you notice the difference in pitch between F# and Gb?

SUPPLEMENTARY TOPICS, CHAPTER II

The C-clef

In addition to the G-clef and the F-clef you may encounter the C-clef, which indicates the position of middle C. The C-clef is most commonly used in the *alto* position, where it points at the center line. Viola players must know this clef, since most of their music is written with it. Sometimes the C-clef will be placed on the 4th line up, in which case it is called the *tenor* clef. Trombone players, bassoonists, and cellists sometimes need to read music written in the tenor clef. Fortunately, you can practice with either of these in *Practica Musica*.

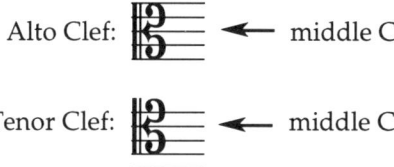

Alto Clef: ← middle C

Tenor Clef: ← middle C

Figure 20: C-clef in alto and tenor positions

Summary, Chapter II

1. Staff notation permits the musician to easily read both rhythm and pitch. The shape of the symbol used tells the rhythmic value of a note and its vertical position on the staff tells its pitch. Each line and space of the 5-line staff corresponds to a white key on the piano.

2. Clefs provide a key to indicate which line or space stands for which note. Today we use most commonly the G-clef (treble clef) which marks the position of the G above middle C, and the F-clef (bass clef) which marks the F below middle C. The *grand staff* is commonly used in piano music; it is a treble and bass clef staff joined together.

3. Writing music out by hand is useful even in the age of computers (your computer is not always with you) and will in any case always be an enjoyable activity. You should develop your ability to write quickly and legibly.

4. *Sharps* and *flats* raise or lower the pitch of a note by one halfstep (a halfstep being the distance from any key to its nearest neighbor). You may also encounter the *double-sharp* and the *double-flat*, which raise or lower a note by two halfsteps. The natural sign cancels any one of these signs.

5. A *key signature* tells you which scale was used to compose a piece of music; it is a collection of flats or sharps that will be used throughout the piece unless cancelled briefly by a natural sign or replaced by another key signature.

6. You can identify the key of a piece by this trick: the last sharp in a sharp key signature is the seventh note of the major scale on which the piece is based, or the second note of the minor scale if the piece is in minor. In a flat key signature the last flat is the fourth note of the major scale or the sixth note of the minor scale.

7. Any natural sign, sharp, or flat that appears in a melody marks a note that is not part of the prevailing major scale or natural minor scale represented by the key signature. Sharps, flats, or naturals used within a measure are known as *accidentals* and are good only until the end of the measure or until cancelled. A *precautionary accidental* is an accidental that isn't really necessary except as a reminder to the reader that an accidental in one of the previous bars is no longer in effect.

Supplementary Topics

8. The *C clef* marks the position of middle C. It is most often seen in the *alto* position, where C is the middle line, and in the *tenor* position, where C is the fourth line up.

III. NOTATION OF RHYTHM

The beat and the measure

If you were inventing your own system of writing music, how would you indicate *when* each note should be played and *how long* it should last?

Modern rhythm notation defines a rhythm by relating it to an imaginary steady pulse or *beat*. For example, some notes may last two beats, some one beat, some only one half beat or less. The beats themselves are counted evenly, like the ticking of a clock, and they are counted in groups called *measures*. The measures are usually of two, three, or four beats, and they might sound like this if you were to count them out loud:

2-beat measures: "One two One two One two One two "

3-beat measures: "One two three One two three One two three"

4-beat measures: "One two three four One two three four"

The larger letters represent *metric accents*. A note played on an accented beat is generally slightly louder or longer than others, or is emphasized in some other way. Usually the first beat of any measure will have the strongest accent, which is called the *primary accent*. Later we'll see that some measures also have a weaker *secondary accent*. For example, 4-beat measures can have a secondary accent on the third beat, like this:

"One two three four One two three four"

Measures are separated in notation by vertical *measure lines* (sometimes these are called *bars* and *barlines*), as in Figure 1, below.

The symbols of rhythm notation

All the symbols for musical notes are derived from the basic one we have already been using, which is called the *wholenote*:

Figure 1: Several wholenotes separated by measure lines

A note half as long as a wholenote is called, of course, a *halfnote*, and it is made by adding a *stem* to the wholenote:

Figure 2: One wholenote is worth two halfnotes

Then we fill in the halfnote to make a *quarternote,* equal in time to one-fourth of a wholenote, add a *flag* to make an *eighthnote,* and then add more and more flags as needed; two flags for a *sixteenthnote,* for example. In theory we could keep adding flags forever and make shorter and shorter notes, but you will rarely see a note shorter than a 64th, which has four flags.

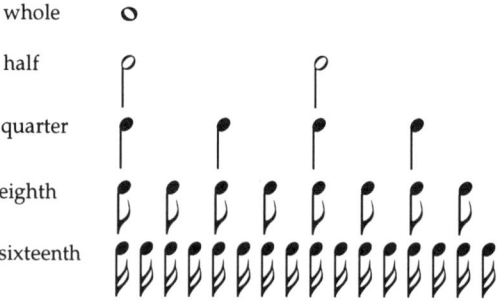

Figure 3: Tree of note values

Beams

Beams are a substitute for flags. You can beam together two or more notes that would otherwise have flags as long as there aren't any unbeamed notes separating them.

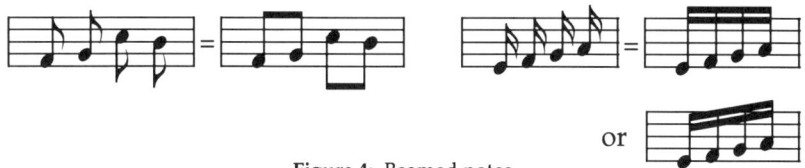

Figure 4: Beamed notes

Dotted notes

A *dot* lengthens a note's value by half. For example, since a quarternote is equal to two eighthnotes, a dotted quarternote will be equal to three eighthnotes. A dotted halfnote is equal to three quarternotes and a dotted eighth to three sixteenths. The dotted note often appears as part of a *dotted pair*, in which it is combined with a short note equal to one-third of its value. Usually the dotted note comes first, as follows:

Figure 5: Dotted pairs (available for listening)

Rests

A *rest* indicates a length of silence. For every note-value there is a corresponding rest:

Figure 6: Table of notes and their equivalent rests

The difference in appearance between the whole rest and the half rest is hard to remember at first. Perhaps it will help if we say that the whole rest symbol fills the top half of a space to show that it has greater value than the half rest, which fills the lower half of a space.

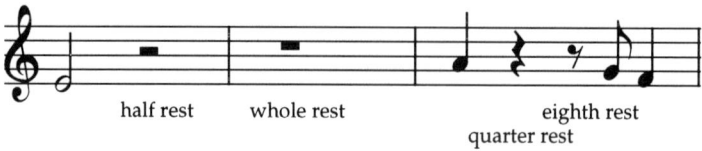

half rest   whole rest   eighth rest
                                          quarter rest

Figure 7: Rests drawn in the staff

Though rests are silent one does continue counting the beat throughout rests — you don't just skip over them! The beat continues at a steady pace through a measure of rests just as it would with notes.

Meter

So far we have discussed only relative note values: we know that a halfnote is half as long as a wholenote, for example, but we don't know how many beats to count for either of them. That information is provided by the *meter signature,* which appears at the beginning of the piece, right after the *clef* and the *key signature:*

Figure 8: Meter signatures

The lower number refers to note type: "4" means quarternotes, for example, while "8" means eighthnotes. The upper number tells you how many beats each bar will have if you count the beat with notes of the given value. Usually you do count the beat with notes of the value given in the lower number of the signature, but there is an exception in the case of *compound meter,* which we'll explain shortly.

A "4/4" signature tells the reader that each measure of the following music will have the same time value as four quarternotes, and it also suggests that each measure will have four beats. It doesn't mean that every measure will necessarily have four actual quarternotes in it — only that the value of the notes in the measure will add up to equal four quarters. For instance, a measure of 4/4 might contain two halfnotes, or three quarters and two eighths, or a single wholenote. And if one quarternote equals one beat in 4/4 time then an eighthnote will last half a beat, a halfnote will last two beats, a wholenote four beats, and so on.

4/4 is probably the most frequent meter in classical and popular music; it is sometimes called *common time*. Another you will often see is 2/2, or *cut time*, which allows the same number of quarternotes in each measure as 4/4 but counts only two beats per bar, so that the halfnotes each get one beat. For this reason cut time (sometimes called *alla breve*) is often used for fast pieces. In cut time an eighthnote lasts only a quarter of a beat, a quarternote is half a beat, and a wholenote is worth two beats.

Usually the meter signature for 4/4 is written not with numbers but with the sign, C, which means the same thing. A "C" with a vertical line through it is used to represent 2/2 (4/4 "cut in half").

Figure 9: Signs for common and cut-time (4/4 and 2/2)

(That "C" does not stand for "common" — it is a remnant of the earliest rhythmic notation. It was originally not a letter C, but a half-circle, and it was used to signify a meter whose beats could be divided in two. A full circle meant that the beat was divisible by three.)

Waltz meter (3/4) is another familiar meter: each measure has three beats, and the beat is counted in quarternotes.

Figure 10: 3/4 meter

The meter signature lasts until the end of the piece or until you change it for a new one — *you don't have to repeat it on every line as you do the clef and key signature.*

11

Activity

Select Melody Writing from your Practica Musica activities menu, and then choose "Write a new melody" from the Melody Writing menu. Practica Musica will then present a staff prepared for the current key and current meter. If the meter is not already 4/4, use the Meter tool (above the keyboard) to choose 4/4. Now write down the following rhythm:

To write notes on the Practica Musica screen just choose the type of note or symbol you want (click one of the boxes in the selection that has appeared over the keyboard) and then click on the staff where you want that symbol to appear. If you put a symbol in the wrong place and need to erase it, first get the Arrow tool by clicking on the Arrow box and then select the symbol you want to erase. Pressing the backspace or delete key will remove the selected symbol.

Now click to turn on the "clapping hands" at the left of the keyboard, and then click on "Play." You'll hear Practica Musica play what you have written while marking the beat in 4/4 time. Notice that the wholenote gets four claps, the halfnotes two, and the quarternotes one each. There are two eighthnotes for each clap.

Try replacing some of the notes with their equivalent rests. Replace as many notes as you like, but be careful to choose the correct equivalent rests so that you still have four beats in every bar.

Once you have the notation correct play the rhythm again and try to clap your hands on each note as Practica Musica marks the beat. Then turn off the clapping hands and mark the beat yourself. Soon you'll understand that the steady beat is the basis of rhythm notation.

Try changing the tempo (command-T). And what happens to the clapping if you change the meter to 2/2?

12

Activity

This would be a good time to try levels 1 and 2 of the Rhythm Matching activity. By learning to repeat rhythms you hear, you will more easily learn to read them later. The rhythms you are asked to repeat will be very simple at first, but they will get more complex as you gain points. Notice that the rhythms are not just drum sounds or the same note repeated; they are brief melodies: when you tap on the letter keys of the computer you'll hear the same pitches as were heard in the model, regardless of what keys you strike! Be sure to tap carefully in time with the clapping hands, so that your own rendition sounds just like what you heard.

Practica Musica is a little bit "forgiving" here, so that your performance does not have to be the exact mathematical equivalent of the original. But you will have to be close enough to show that you do understand the pattern.

Simple and compound meter

Simple meters are those in which the beat is represented by a plain undotted note. All the meters we have seen so far are simple: 2/2, 2/4, 3/4, and 4/4. In simple meters the upper number of the meter signature tells the number of beats per bar and the lower number identifies the note that is equal to one beat.

In *compound* meters the beat is represented by a dotted note, which means that the meter signature is interpreted a little differently. For example, according to our previous definition "6/8" does mean that there would be six beats to the bar if you counted one beat for each eighthnote, but in fact musicians usually count only two beats in a 6/8 bar, so that each beat is as long as one dotted quarternote (remember that one dotted quarternote is equal to three eighthnotes). 9/8 is treated the same way: if you were tapping your foot you'd tap it three times in each 9/8 measure, again beating the time of dotted quarters.

This familiar melody should give you the feel for 6/8:

The   it- sy bit- sy   spi- der ran   up   the wa- ter   spout

beats: 1   2   1   2   1   2   1

Figure 11: The beat pattern of a fast 6/8 (available for listening)

How can you tell if a meter is compound? It depends both on how the music is written and how it is performed. If the notes of each measure seem to be grouped into threes, with each group being fast enough to seem like a single beat, then the meter is compound. One giveaway is the sight of a dotted note that is followed by another dotted note instead of being part of a "dotted pair." That may imply that the beat is moving with the dotted notes, as in this example of a compound 9/4:

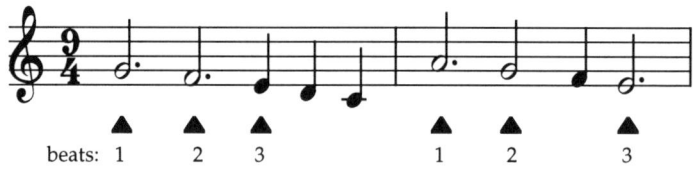

beats: 1   2   3   1   2   3

Figure 12: A compound 9/4

13

Activity

Go to the Melody Writing/Listening activity and open the musical example for Figure 11, above (it will be in the Melodies folder, under the name "Chapter 03, Figure 11."

Use the "Play" button to listen to this example. Can you clap along with the beat? If you cannot, turn on the clapping hands and try clapping along with Practica Musica as the melody plays, demonstrating that there are two beats in each of these 6/8 measures. Play it again and try singing the words (no need to be shy).

(cont'd)

Once you have the Itsy-Bitsy Spider well in hand, go to the "custom level" in Rhythm Matching. Set the difficulty button to the first, or easiest, position, and then choose 6/8 from the meter menu so that all the examples given you will sound in 6/8 time. These are invented by the program as it goes along, so you won't run out of examples. After you hear each pattern you'll be asked to tap the rhythm. Within a short time you should have the "feel" of 6/8 meter. Try it at different speeds (tempo can be changed with command-T) and then do the same exercise with 9/8.

Beaming with a purpose

Now that you know the importance of the beat in rhythm notation you can appreciate that beams are best used to group notes together to make the beats clear to the eye of the reader:

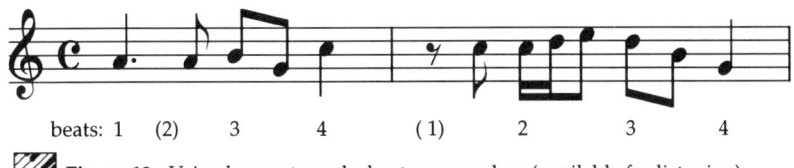

beats: 1   (2)   3   4   (1)   2   3   4

Figure 13: Using beams to make beat groups clear (available for listening)

The following notation would sound the same as the above example if played by a computer, but it makes little sense visually and would make very hard reading for a human:

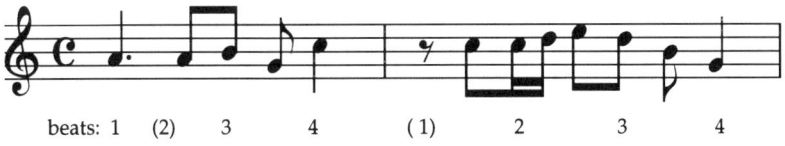

beats: 1   (2)   3   4   (1)   2   3   4

Figure 14: An incorrectly beamed measure (available for listening)

Beaming in 6/8 and 3/4

Music in 6/8, if beamed incorrectly, may look like it's really in 3/4. In 6/8 performed with two beats to the bar you must be careful to beam your eighthnotes in threes instead of twos, unless you are deliberately making a special effect. Otherwise you could accidentally give the impression of three beats to the bar. Incorrect beaming could cause a musician to confuse the performance by putting the accents in the wrong places. The following two examples have exactly the same notes and note values, but they would sound different if well-performed:

Figure 15: Beams help to show the difference between 3/4 and 6/8
(available for listening)

14

Activity

Again using Practica Musica's Melody Writing/Listening activity, open the musical example for Figure 15, above (its name will be "Chapter 03, Figure 15." With the clapping hands turned on, listen to both the 3/4 and the 6/8 version.

How different the two performances sound, though they have the same notes! The computer does not accent the notes as a human would, but the clapping gives the impression of an accent on each beat, allowing you to get some idea of the difference. You can improve the distinction by singing along with the computer: for the 3/4, sing " ba-la, ba-la, ba-la," for the 6/8, sing "ba-la-la, ba-la-la."

Stem direction

Stems can go either up or down. Either way the note will sound the same, but the choice of stem direction may be important for visual clarity. If you have only one line of music on a staff then the stem direction depends on position: notes above the middle of the staff have their stems down and those on the middle line or below have their stems up. *Notice that descending stems are always on the left side of the note head and ascending ones are always on the right:*

Figure 16: Notes with varying stem direction

Notice also that *flags always wave to the right, regardless of stem direction.* You might just imagine that the wind always blows from the left side of the page!

Sometimes composers use stem direction to show that certain notes belong together or are sung by the same voice. In that case they will ignore the rule about staff position and just make one singer's notes all with upward stems and another singer's notes all with downward stems, and so on. In this music for soprano, alto, tenor, and bass, the soprano's notes have upward stems, the alto's downward, the tenor upward again, and the bass downward:

Figure 17: Stem direction separates voices in this Bach Chorale

SUPPLEMENTARY TOPICS, CHAPTER III

Asymmetrical meter

All of the meters discussed so far are based on beat groupings that divide in either threes or twos: the *duple meters* divide in 2 (2/4, 2/2, 4/4, 6/8 etc); the *triple* meters divide in threes (3/2, 3/4, 9/8). On occasion you'll encounter music written in a meter that does not divide evenly by either three or two, such as 5/4 or 7/4 or 7/8. Such meters are rare in classical music, but have often been used in our own century by both "serious" and pop musicians. Familiar examples are Dave Brubeck's *Take Five*, in 5/4 time, and the Beatles' *All you need is love*, much of which is in 7/4.

These asymmetrical meters are not as hard to perform as they might seem at first glance. The trick is to consider each measure as a combination of smaller regular beat groups. 5/4, for example, can be regarded as 2/4 + 3/4 or 3/4 + 2/4 (depending on the music — this is a matter of interpretation). 7/4 has more possibilities — it might seem to written as 4/4 + 3/4, or 3/4 + 2/4 + 2/4, etc. Musicians often work out their interpretation of such meters bar by bar and then think of them that way while playing:

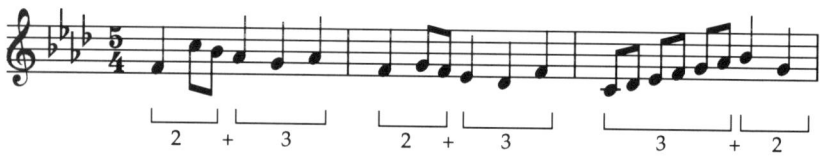

Figure 18: Metric groupings in a 5/4 melody (available for listening)

Keeping notation simple

If you are writing down a rhythm to be played on an instrument whose sound stops quickly, such as a wood block or a snare drum, the use of rests is uncertain. For example, the following four patterns will all sound the same when played by a wood block:

Figure 19: Four patterns that could sound the same

Musicians generally prefer to keep notation as simple as possible, and so a composer wanting short notes on a wood block would probably choose (2) or even (1) as the way to notate this pattern. Both performances would sound the same, and either one would be easier to write and read than (3) or (4). On the other hand, if the instrument were a violin each of these patterns would sound different, with long notes in (1) and very short notes in (4).

Notation does not tell you everything about how a passage will sound; you need to consider also what instrument is being used — as well as the tempo, the style of the piece, and other subtle factors.

Summary, Chapter III

1. Rhythmic notation is based on the concept of a steady underlying *beat*. Beats are grouped into *measures* of one, two, three, four, or more beats, the first of which is more prominent than the others. Some meters also have a secondary accent on one of the other beats: 4/4 has a secondary accent on the third beat.

2. The basic note value is the *wholenote*, which can be divided into two *halfnotes* or four *quarternotes* or eight *eighthnotes*, etc. The note values are distinguished by the symbol being filled-in or hollow, by the presence or absence of a *stem* and the presence or absence of one or more *flags*.

3. A *dot* after a note increases its value by one half, e.g., a dotted quarternote is as long as a quarternote plus an eighth-note.

4. The flags found on notes shorter than the quarternote may sometimes be replaced by *beams*, which help to group notes in a way that makes the beat easier to see.

5. For every note-value there is a corresponding *rest*, which just indicates a length of silence.

6. The *meter signature* at the beginning of a piece describes how its beats are grouped and also tells which note value is equal to one beat. The lower number refers to note value: "4" means "quarternote," for example. The upper number tells you how many beats each measure will have if you count one beat for each of the given note values.

7. *Simple* meters are those in which the beat is counted with undotted notes; in *compound* meters the beat is counted with dotted notes. In a compound meter the upper number of the signature equals three times the actual number of beats in the bar. 2/2, 4/4, 3/4, and 4/8 are all simple meters; 6/8 and 9/8 are usually performed as compound meters.

8. Stems may go either up or down without affecting the rhythm. Usually notes above the middle line of a staff have their stems downward; notes on or below the middle line have their stems upward.

Supplementary Topics

9. *Asymmetrical* meters are those that divide neither by two nor three, such as 5/4 and 7/8. It is best to think of these as a combination of duple and triple meters — for instance, 5/4 can be read as 2/4 + 3/4 or 3/4 + 2/4, depending on the rhythmic groups within each measure.

IV. READING RHYTHM

Counting beats

There are several ways that you can help yourself when trying to read an unfamiliar rhythm. One of them is to "count" the beats aloud or in your head. You can give a number to each beat and subdivide it as in the examples below. Figure 1 demonstrates counting with the beat subdivided in halves:

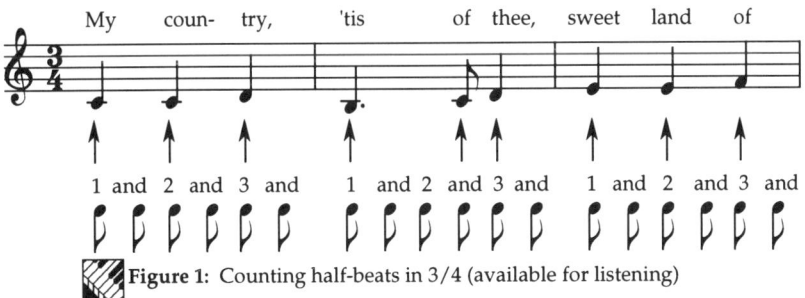

Figure 1: Counting half-beats in 3/4 (available for listening)

If there are sixteenthnotes in the music you can add two more syllables and count the beat divided in fours, again speaking each syllable at a steady rate, like the ticking of a clock. For example:

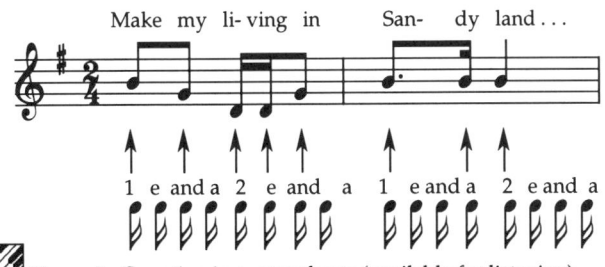

Figure 2: Counting in quarter-beats (available for listening)

Since each beat of a compound meter divides in three parts you could count a 6/8 measure with "One-two-three, Two-two-three," like this:

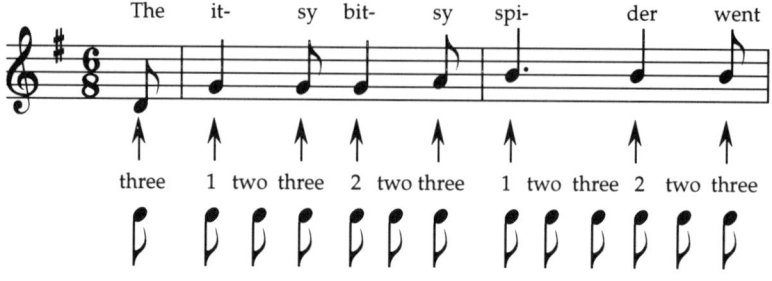

Figure 3: Counting beats that divide in three
(available for listening in Chapter II, Figure 11)

The basic principle of rhythmic counting is to count steadily at the speed of the shortest note in the melody, and to use numbers to identify each beat. The actual syllables you speak don't matter, of course: for beats divided in two or three as above you could just as easily say "One wump Two wump" and "One bop bop Two bop bop." All that matters is that the counts are evenly spaced. Nor do you have to count out loud: the counting can be all in your head. Eventually you won't need to count at all.

We'll use Figure 4 to show how you would work out the counting for a typical melody. In this example there are three beats to a bar, each equal to a quarternote (we can tell that from the meter signature) and the shortest note is an eighth. An eighthnote is therefore one-half a beat, so we'll divide each beat into two equally-spaced syllables. A halfnote is worth four eighthnotes, so it will receive four syllables:

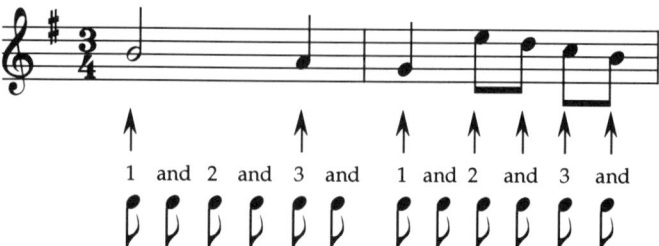

Figure 4: Counting in 3/4 time

Mental conducting

Another help in reading rhythm is to "conduct" the music in your imagination. In fact, even when you already understand the rhythm mental conducting is a good way to keep your place without losing the beat. Before trying mental conducting you should practice some actual conducting movements, as follows.

Try swinging your arm loosely from side from side, noticing how it accelerates into the bottom of the swing and slows down as it approaches the top of each swing, just like a pendulum. Once your arm is swinging in a relaxed and free manner, slowly bring your wrist up by bending your elbow and reduce the movement until only your forearm is swinging back and forth from left to right — with a downward emphasis on the outward swing. Now you are beating the time in two, as in 2/2 or 2/4, or 6/8 (remember that 6/8 usually has two beats per measure).

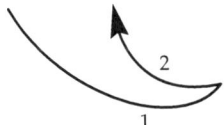

Figure 5: Conducting pattern for two beats to the bar

You can use a similar motion of the arm to swing into these other patterns, which indicate 3 and 4 beats per measure (the illustrations are for the right arm — everything is reversed if you are lefthanded):

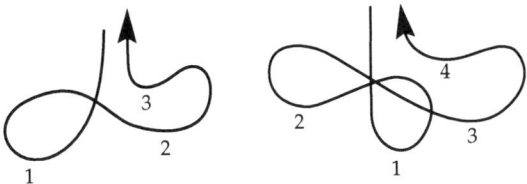

Figure 6: Conducting in three and in four.

The numbers in the drawings are placed roughly at the "bottom" of the swings to show you that there's a slight downward emphasis marking each beat. Remember also that the drawings are only approximate!

15

Activity

Choose Melody Writing from your Practica Musica Activity menu, and then select "Write a melody" from the Melody Writing menu. Then pick the key of F major from the Key list above the keyboard, and choose the meter 3/4 from the meter list. You have had a little practice in using the editing features of Practica Musica, so you should be able to enter on the staff the notes of this melody, which comes from Beethoven's Second Symphony:

After entering the notes, press the Autostem and Autobeam buttons to make the melody look as it does above. (On your Practica Musica screen all the above will be on one line).

From the meter signature of 3/4 you can tell that each measure has three beats and that the beats move at the speed of quarter notes. Play the melody with the clapping hands turned on, and conduct it in 3/4 as you listen, making sure that you are conducting at the same speed as the hands are clapping. Then turn off the metronome and conduct the piece without guidance. You can also try the melody at different speeds: use the "Set Tempo" option (Sound Options, or command-T).

Of course it doesn't matter how you conduct — the machine will play the same anyway! — but it's good practice in learning the conducting patterns and it helps you learn to follow a musical score.

(cont'd)

Next, try counting in quick sixteenth-notes as you conduct, using "One-e-and-a Two-e-and-a Three-e-and-a," etc. Most of the notes are quarternotes, and so they get four syllables. If you have trouble with the counting try using the "Set Tempo" menu choice to slow down the melody.

After this task grows easy you might try conducting melodies generated by the computer. You can never tell what these will be like; they are new every time. Choose Pitch Dictation from the Activity menu and select the Custom Level of generated melodies. Each time you click on the "New" button above the keyboard Practica Musica will invent a new melody that uses whatever meter you last chose from the meter list (you can change key, too). Note that the melody will not appear on the screen until you press the "evaluate" button.

More on metric accents

In Chapter III we mentioned that different meters can be recognized by their metric accents. Each measure begins with a strong *primary accent* on its first beat and certain meters can also have a weaker *secondary accent*, such as the secondary accent on the third beat in 4/4.

The metric accents are a natural consequence of repeated patterns. Suppose, for example, that you try saying the numbers "one two three four" out loud for a while, keeping a steady rhythm as if you were counting beats. Your counting will probably start to sound like this, sooner or later:

$$1 \; {}_2 \; 3 \; {}_4 \; 1 \; {}_2 \; 3 \; {}_4 \; 1 \; {}_2 \; 3 \; {}_4$$

The largest numerals represent the primary accent, the midsized numerals the *secondary accent*, and the smallest ones (2 and 4 in 4/4 time) mark the *weak beats*.

Depending on your listening habits, you might also find yourself falling into the reverse of the above. Rock music often tends to emphasize the weak beats:

$$_1\,\mathbf{2}\,_3\,\mathbf{4}\,_1\,\mathbf{2}\,_3\,\mathbf{4}\,!!$$

This off-center emphasis of rock does not actually change the strong nature of the first and third beats, however. It's really a kind of *syncopation* (see the next chapter), which gives a special emphasis to weak beats with the understanding that they will still be perceived as weak. Pop musicians sometimes refer to these "misplaced" accents as *backbeat*. So the melody is designed to have its important notes on the strong beats, while the accompaniment emphasizes the two and four, as in this typical rock tune:

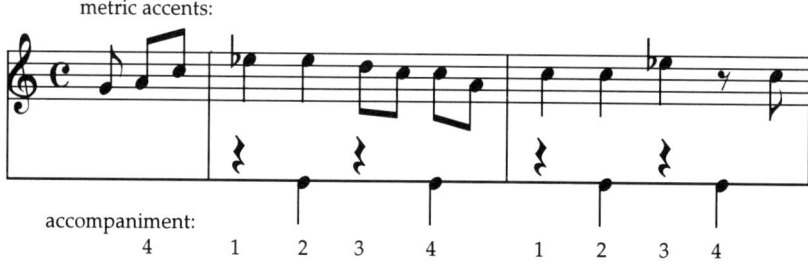

Figure 7: Weak beat emphasis in rock accompaniment

No matter what sort of music you listen to, it will be difficult to avoid falling into the following pattern when counting three-beat measures:

$$\mathbf{1}\,_2\,_3\,\mathbf{1}\,_2\,_3\,\mathbf{1}\,_2\,_3\,\mathbf{1}\,_2\,_3$$

In a *triple meter* like this one both the second and third beats are weak.

If you compare these emphasis patterns to the conducting patterns you'll see that conducting expresses visually the same metric accents. This is most obvious in a simple two-beat, where the outward and downward swing of the hand has stronger character than the inward and upward swing — it represents the stronger *downbeat* while the return of the hand marks the weak *upbeat*.

In a four-beat conducting pattern there is a similar emphasis: the long motion from left to right tends to give the "three" almost as much weight as the "one," dividing the measure into two halves of two beats each. When conducting in three-four, on the other hand, the measure doesn't seem to divide in any way except in three. In all the patterns the "one" has what seems like the greatest importance, and the last beat of the measure is a preparation for the next "one."

Be careful not to overdo metric accents; they will come naturally without much deliberate effort to produce them. The accented note doesn't have to be louder than the others — it might only be held a little longer — and you may want in some cases to avoid obvious accents altogether. Sometimes the accents are indicated well enough by the harmonic accompaniment (perhaps a new chord will be played on the accented notes). One way or another, however, the metric accents should be communicated because they give each meter its character; they are part of the reason why a musician can hear that a piece is in three-four rather than six-eight without seeing the music.

As an example of the effect of meter on a melodic pattern let's look at the metric accents in two different versions of the same melody, the same melody that was used in Chapter III to illustrate the need for careful use of beams. This tune would be conducted in three beats if written in 3/4, and its accents would fall on the first note of each pair, especially the first note of the measure, which carries the primary accent:

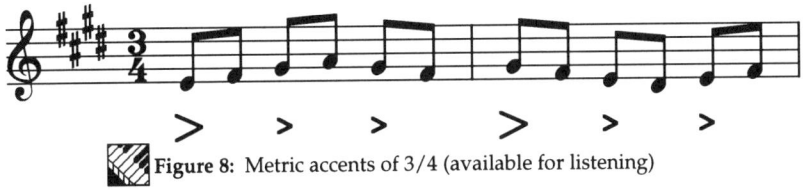

Figure 8: Metric accents of 3/4 (available for listening)

The choice of "important notes" would come out differently in a 6/8 version of the same pattern, which would be conducted in two instead of three:

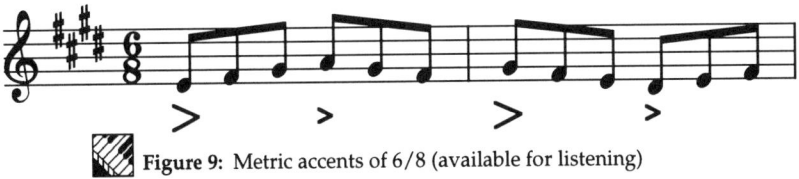

Figure 9: Metric accents of 6/8 (available for listening)

The computer, unfortunately, plays these examples both the same, since it doesn't have the flexibility to interpret metric accents properly, despite the fact that you can give some impression of metric accent by turning on the clapping hands metronome. The machine could be programmed to make the accented notes always louder, but that would get tiresome. Making them always longer would also get old after a while. A human musician considers the desired expression, the speed of performance, the way the melody is moving, the nature of the accompaniment, the phrasing — and then adjusts in whatever way will make that particular piece most effective. The only way to learn that art is by listening to good performers. Which brings us to the topic of music that goes....

Beyond the written note

It's important to remember that the notation of rhythm, like all music notation, is not meant to be a complete mathematical description of the sound — a complete description would be very complicated and hard to read. Written music requires some additional interpretation. Great performers rarely play the same piece twice in the same way, yet all their performances are correct readings; what we are doing now is *just the first step* — learning to understand the basic design provided by the notation.

The additions made in interpretation are often subtle and may take experience to appreciate fully. In a group of quarter notes that all look the same on the page some may be played with more "air" between them, a variation that falls under the heading of change in *articulation*. And there may sometimes be a certain freedom with the tempo, which is known as *rubato* and which may include speeding up (*accelerando*) or slowing down (*ritardando*). A note may sometimes be brought into prominence by an *agogic accent* — an accent produced by playing the note a tiny bit early or late (the word *agogic* refers to all accents made by changes in note length or timing). And here we're only speaking of rhythmic variation; there are many other ways that two performances can vary without either being incorrect.

An easy-to-hear example of rhythmic freedom is found in most performances of the beginning of the *Blue Danube* waltz by Johann Strauss. The *rubato* described below does not appear in the score but almost everyone plays it that way, and it works very well:

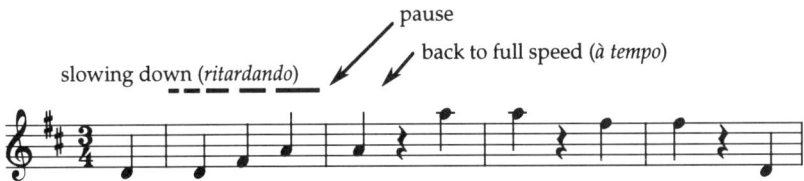

Figure 10: On the Beautiful Blue Danube

That graceful slowing to a pause, followed by a return to the normal tempo, gives an effect that might be compared to coasting over the top of a hill on a bicycle: just briefly one reaches a point of stillness, and then movement starts again. It's perfect for an invitation to a dance, and this interpretation has become a tradition with Viennese waltz music.

16

Activity

The Rhythm Reading activity is designed to give you practice in reading the rhythm of a tune without your having to think about reading its pitches. You will hear the correct pitches automatically as you tap the rhythm, which makes the game more fun.

Select Rhythm Reading, Level 1, from your Practica Musica Activities menu. The metronome will begin clapping as you examine the notes on the screen. Take your time and think the rhythm to yourself before actually striking the keys of the computer. Keep in careful time with the metronome.

If you didn't get full points for your performance, be sure to play the notation that Practica Musica displayed as "your version." This represents the best job the program could do at putting what you played into notation. Listen to both your version and the original. Can you hear the difference?

Be sure to finish Level 1 before you go on to Level 2, even if you find the first examples easy - they will get more difficult as you gain points. You'll need to read Chapter V before trying levels 3 and 4.

17

Activity

Once you can read the rhythms of levels 1 and 2 you should attempt doing the opposite task: writing down a rhythm that you hear. The RhythmDictation activity will present short melodies whose rhythm you can write in the staff, using the note editing tools. You'll find that the pitches are automatic —! — all you need to do is to choose the correct note and rest values and put them in order on the staff. You should also enter barlines as needed. Try a few of the library melodies for each of the first two levels, but don't neglect to do generated tunes. The generated melodies are certain to be unfamiliar and always fresh. Once you can do some of these you will not only understand notation better, but you will have taken the first steps in learning to write music by ear.

SUPPLEMENTARY TOPICS, CHAPTER IV

Conducting asymmetrical meters

To conduct an asymmetrical meter you need to think about how the rhythm works within each measure. For example, 5/4 can be 2 + 3 or 3+2:

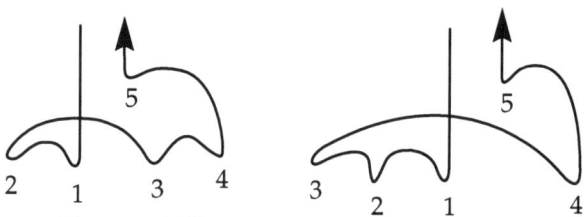

Figure 11: Different ways of beating a 5/4 measure.

As in the other conducting diagrams, these illustrations are only approximate! A conductor has considerable freedom of movement.

Summary, Chapter IV

1. Counting the beats out loud or in your head is one way to learn an unfamiliar rhythm. It helps to subdivide each beat into halves, quarters, or thirds, as appropriate. Beats can be counted in halves using the syllable "and" for the half-beats: "One and Two and Three and Four and." In a compound meter each beat can be divided in threes by saying, "One two three Two two three, etc." You can further divide either of the above by adding one more syllable: "One-e-and-a two-e-and-a three-e-and-a four-e-and-a" for beats divided in four parts or "One-a two-a three-a Two-a two-a Three-a" for beats divided in six parts.

2. The conducting patterns will also guide you in understanding rhythm. They help you to keep your place and also indicate the metric accents of each meter.

3. Music in 4/4 time has a primary accent on the first beat and a secondary accent on the third beat, while 3/4 accents just the first beat. 6/8 meter is conducted in two, like 2/4, so it has its primary accent on the first beat; it may also have a secondary accent at the beginning of the second beat if the melody is moving in eighthnotes. These metric accents are shown sometimes by greater loudness, sometimes by greater length of accented notes, sometimes just in the accompaniment. Sometimes the accompaniment will contrast the accents of the meter, as in rock music.

4. Written music requires interpretation — the printed music is not a literal transcription. An understanding of performance traditions is needed to perform written music well.

Supplementary Topics

5. Reading an asymmetrical meter is easier if you group its beats into threes and twos. These submetrical groupings are reflected in the usual conducting patterns for asymmetrical meters.

V. COMPLEX RHYTHM

The tie

The *tie* joins two notes of the same pitch so that they sound like one. Sometimes you can use a tie to mean the same thing as a dot:

Figure 1: A tie can be used instead of a dot

The tie can also be used to make notes of a length that can't be created with dots, such as a quarter note plus a sixteenth. And a tie is the only way to hold a note over a bar line:

Figure 2: In some places only a tie will do

Another important purpose of the tie is to make the beat groupings clear within a measure:

is easier to read if written this way:

beats: 1   2   3   4

Figure 3: Using a tie to make beat groups clear

Activity   **18**

Select Melody Writing from your Practica Musica Activities menu and then select "Write a new melody" from the Melody Writing menu. Choose the key of D major and the meter 4/4. Now enter the melody below:

Play the above tune to hear what it sounds like, then put in the following ties so that you can hear what ties will do.

To tie notes follow this procedure:

1) Select the arrow tool by clicking in the arrow box.
2) Drag a selection rectangle to select both notes to be tied. Or hold click on the first note, hold down the shift key, and click on the second one.
4) With the notes selected, click on the tie button in the keyboard tools.

tie button

 Try playing the tied melody with the clapping hands turned on! With the beat marked you can more clearly hear the effect of these ties.

Syncopation

Syncopation is something you probably know well without being aware of it. It gives vivacity to rhythm and is an important part of jazz and popular music, as well as being a frequent device in the classics. To syncopate you just begin a note on an "offbeat" (anywhere other than the beginning of a beat) and carry it over to the next beat. It creates an effect that might be described as "starting the note early."

Figure 4: Examples of syncopation (available for listening)

Usually the word "syncopation" refers to notes that are held over as above. But in a more general sense any rhythm that emphasizes the offbeats could be called "syncopated:"

Figure 5: Syncopated notes that aren't held over (available for listening)

When syncopated notes are held over to the next beat the beat groups will be easier to see if you use ties. But simple patterns such as syncopated quarter notes are so common that they are often written without ties. So sometimes you have a choice of ways to write the syncopated passage:

Figure 6: Two ways of notating the same thing (available for listening)

19

Activity

Select Pitch Dictation from your Practica Musica Activities menu and then select "Custom generated melodies." Pick the "most difficult" level, and set the melody length to 8 beats. After clicking OK, click the "Evaluate" button so that you can see the melody invented by Practica Musica. Most of the generated tunes at this level will have at least some syncopation. Do you see any syncopation in this one? If you don't, click "New" until the machine comes up with a syncopated melody.

Turn on the clapping hands and try to conduct the melody as Practica Musica plays it for you. Then turn off the clapping hands and try to do the clapping yourself, marking the beat in 4/4 time (the melody will have been created using 4/4 meter unless you requested otherwise). Once you can easily follow the rhythm while clapping the beat, press "New" again and try it with a new melody.

20

Activity

Select Rhythm Matching from the Activities menu. If you have already graduated from levels 1 and 2 this would be a good time to try Level 3, which sometimes involves syncopation. Remember that Practica Musica will automatically provide the pitches for you in the rhythm exercises: you need concern yourself only with choosing the correct rhythmic values. Practica Musica will understand if you use two tied short notes instead of one long one, or vice-versa, and it is fairly flexible in some other ways, too. If your version sounds essentially like the model then you will earn points.

Once you can match the rhythms you hear, try reading them in Level 3 of Rhythm Reading. The last and most difficult step will be writing down such rhythms by ear, which you can attempt in Level 3 of Rhythm Dictation.

SUPPLEMENTARY TOPICS, CHAPTER V.

Hemiola

Hemiola is a special kind of syncopation. You could use this term for any syncopation that causes the effect of duple meter within the context of triple meter, or vice-versa. In both of the following examples the second measure uses hemiola: in the first case three quarternotes are played in the time of two beats (remember that 6/8 has two beats to the bar); in the second example two dotted quarters are played in the time of three beats.

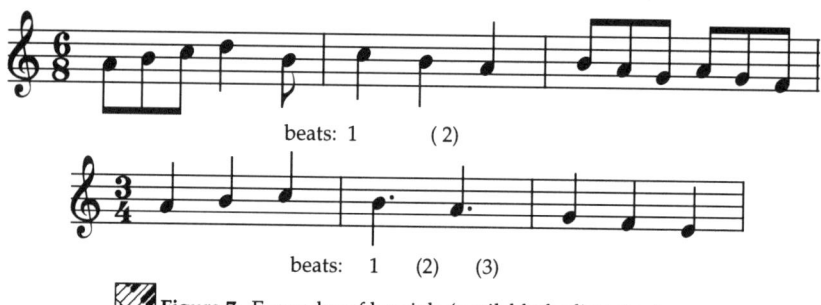

Figure 7: Examples of hemiola (available for listening)

Triplets, duplets, and tuplets

Perhaps you've noticed that all undotted notes divide only in twos, fours, eights, etc. What if you want to fit three equal notes into the time of a single undotted quarter-note?

You can do it by marking each group with the number "3," as follows:

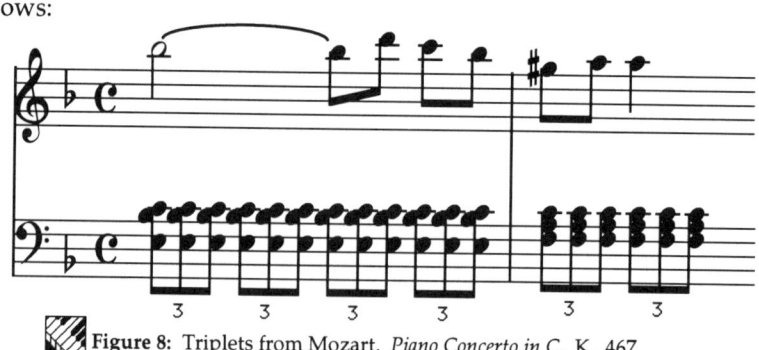

Figure 8: Triplets from Mozart, *Piano Concerto in C*, K. 467

The grouping is called a *triplet*, and it is most effective when used as Mozart uses it above, in contrast to duple rhythm. The "3" means that three notes are to be played in the time of two. In the Mozart, three triplet eighthnotes are played in the time of two normal eighthnotes, i.e., in the time of a quarternote. The below illustration shows how you would notate triplets having the time value of a halfnote, a quarternote, or an eighthnote:

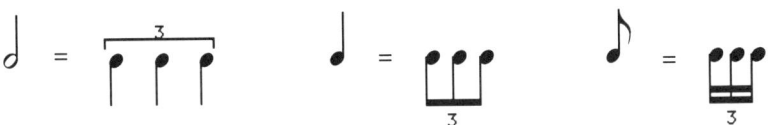

Figure 9: Triplets in 4rs, 8ths, 16ths

Contrasting the triplet is the *duplet*, an occasion where you play only two equal notes in the time of what would be three:

Figure 10: A duplet

That duplet rhythm could be notated literally, using dotted notes:

Figure 11: Another way to notate the same rhythm (available for listening)

You could also write five eighth notes to fit in the time of four normal eighth notes, and mark this *quintuplet* with a "5":

Figure 12: A quintuplet (available for listening)

Many musicians have simply adopted the word *tuplet* as a general term for all irregular groups other than the triplet. The performance of large tuplets can sometimes be flexible. Here's a very large irregular grouping by Chopin:

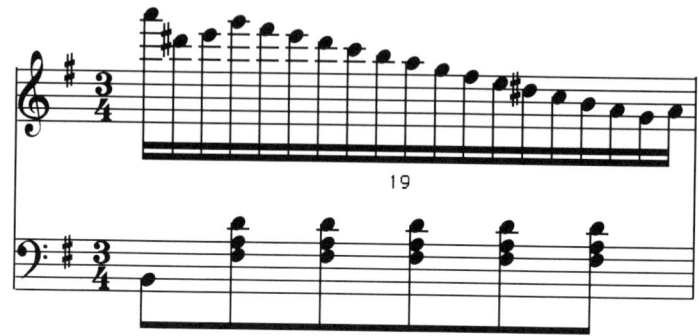

Figure 13: 19-note tuplet in Chopin's Piano Concerto in E Minor

Naturally he didn't really expect the musician to play 19 notes in mathematically exact time! What he intended was that the pianist should use a free, improvisatory style for these notes. But smaller groups like triplets really must be precise for a good effect.

Summary, Chapter V

1. A *tie* joins two notes so that they sound like one. Ties can be used to hold notes over a bar line, to make notes of a length that can't be made with dots, such as a quarter plus a sixteenth, and also to visually clarify the beat groups in a measure.

2. *Syncopated* notes are those that begin offbeat and avoid any accent on the downbeat.

Supplementary Topics

3. *Hemiola* is a type of syncopation that causes the effect of duple meter within the context of triple meter, or vice-versa.

4. A *triplet* is a group of three notes that sounds in the time allotted for two. It is marked with a "3." Similarly, a *duplet* is a group of two notes that sounds in the time that would normally be taken by three. *Tuplet* is a general term for other irregular groupings, such as the *quintuplet*.

VI. EXPRESSION MARKS

In this chapter we'll cover various of the expression marks that are used to provide extra information about the way a passage is to be played. The expression marks are "extras" — they don't have to be there but are often helpful. They are relatively new in music notation — composers before the late 18th century rarely indicated much more than the plain notes. Nonetheless, editors often add them to older pieces as suggestions for the performer.

Signs affecting articulation

The *staccato* sign is a dot placed below the note head, or above it if the stem is downward. It tells the musician to play this note clearly separated from the next one. Often this is misinterpreted to mean that a staccato note should be as short as possible, but really it just means to put a little "air" between the notes — however much is necessary to give the effect. How much separation is necessary is a matter concerning which honest musicians may differ. Staccato can even be put on notes of long value, such as half notes:

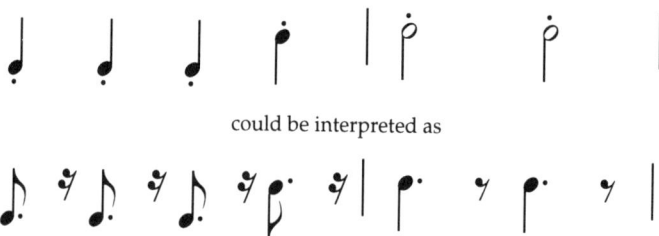

could be interpreted as

Figure 1: Staccato notes and an interpretation

If you want to emphasize that certain notes are *very* short you should combine a shorter note value with the staccato sign:

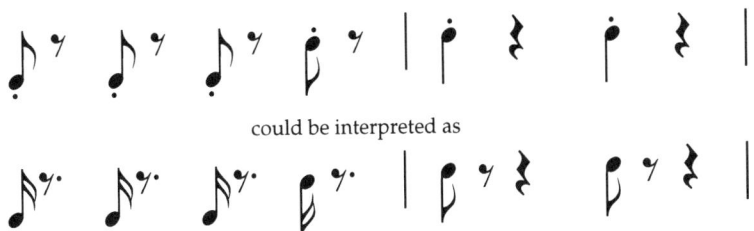

could be interpreted as

Figure 2: Shorter staccato notes and an interpretation

The opposite of staccato is *tenuto* (tenOOtow), which just means "held out." The tenuto sign is a horizontal line, written in the same place as the staccato sign. Often it carries an additional meaning of a certain emphasis to be given the marked notes:

Figure 3: The tenuto sign

Accent

An accent mark is a short horizontal wedge over a note head, >, meaning that the note should be played especially vigorously. Another way to indicate the same thing is the sign *sf*, which stands for *sforzando*, meaning "forced."

Figure 4: Two ways of marking an accent

Dynamics

Indications of loud and soft are easy to understand once you know that *forte* means loud and *piano* means soft. Just remember that our keyboard instrument called the "piano" got its name from being able to play both soft and loud (*piano* is short for *pianoforte*). *Forte* is abbreviated *f* and *piano* is abbreviated *p*.

All the other dynamic markings are built from these: *ff* (*fortissimo*, or very loud), *mf* (*mezzo-forte*, or moderately loud), *mp* (*mezzo-piano*, or moderately quiet), and *pp* (*pianissimo*, or very quiet). Sometimes you'll see further extremes like *fff* or *ppp*, but it doesn't make much sense to keep on adding f's and p's beyond three. Aaron Copland once wrote *ppppp* under a very high note in music for a flute, but he was probably just making a little joke (it's very difficult to play a high note quietly on a flute).

ppp   pp   p   mp   mf   f   ff   fff

←——— quieter   louder ———→

Figure 5: Indications of dynamics

Crescendo and decrescendo

A gradual *crescendo* (a getting louder) can be indicated by either the abbreviation, "cresc." or by a graphic symbol, ⎯⎯. *Decrescendo* is just the opposite: ⎯⎯. You may also see the words *diminuendo* (diminishing) or *morendo* (dying away) used for a decrescendo. Don't confuse the decrescendo with the short accent mark ⟩.

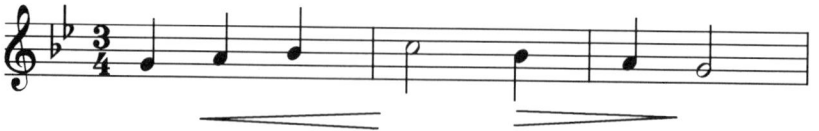

Figure 6: *Crescendo* and *decrescendo* or *diminuendo*

Slurs and phrasing marks

The *slur* looks like the *tie*, except that it connects two or more notes of different pitch. The effect is to make the notes *legato*, or smoothly joined together. A violinist will avoid lifting the bow between slurred notes; a performer on a wind instrument will do them in the same breath without retonguing. On the piano, legato notes are joined by holding the first one until the next one begins.

A *phrase mark* looks like a very long slur, except that you aren't really expected to play all the notes within it slurred together: the mark only suggests that these notes should be thought of as part of the same musical idea. The end of a phrase is often marked by performers with a "taking of a breath:" a drop in loudness, a short rest, or even a very slight pause in the counting of time. Phrase marks cover more than a single measure, while most slurs connect just a few notes. If you see a phrase mark in a classical work from the time of Mozart and Beethoven it is probably an editorial suggestion — composers of that era generally left phrasing up to the performer. Even today performers will find their own ways of phrasing a piece unless the composer's intentions are unequivocal.

Figure 7: Slurs and a phrase mark.

Tempo indications

The speed, or *tempo*, of a piece is traditionally indicated in Italian using such terms as *allegro* (fast), *andante* (walking), *adagio*, (slow) and so on. Many of these terms have colorings to their meaning that go beyond mere speed of execution, however. For example, *adagio* is not only slow but sad, whereas *maestoso* is slow but stately and positive. Sometimes a certain musical effect or figure is associated with a tempo indication: *maestoso* will often feature dotted rhythms implying a ceremonial procession, whereas *andante* often involves steady ("walking") eighth-notes in the bass. *Allegro* is frequently not only fast but hopeful, positive, or even heroic, whereas *presto* is fast and just exciting, sometimes in a lighter mood.

Composers since the time of Beethoven often add a metronome mark as well, which is a precise measure of beats per minute. But the metronome mark lacks the emotional associations mentioned above. Metronome rates are measured as ticks per minute; a marking of ♩ = 50 means fifty quarter notes to the minute.

These are the most common of the tempo indications:

Slow to moderate: *largo* , *lento* , *adagio* , *andante*

Moderate to very fast: *moderato, allegretto, allegro, presto*

SUPPLEMENTARY TOPICS, CHAPTER VI.

Other Italian words used to indicate expression

We can add to the above list a few words that will give you a clue to the meaning of other common indications:

brio = brilliance.
con = with.   Example: *Allegro con brio*
non = not.
troppo = too much.
ma = but.   Example: *Allegro, ma non troppo*
molto = very much.
-issimo = (suffix meaning 'very much').
sempre = always.   Example: *Sempre molto fortissimo*
y = and.

Summary, Chapter VI.

1. The expressive signs provide information that often would be provided by the interpretive skill of the performer. They are generally used only when a composer wants to make especially sure that the performer will play a passage in a certain way.

2. The *staccato* sign indicates that a note is to be clearly separated from the following note. This generally has the effect of making the note sound short. The sign for staccato is a dot placed above or below a note head, depending on the stem direction.

3. The *tenuto* sign, a short line placed above or below the note head, indicates that the note should be held out as long as possible (but without actually joining it to the next note).

4. The accent mark, $>$, means that a note is to be played especially vigorously.

5. Dynamics are indicated by the abbreviations of the Italian words *pianissimo, piano, mezzopiano, mezzoforte, forte, fortissimo: pp, p, mp, mf, f, ff.*

6. Increasing loudness, or crescendo, is indicated by the word *cresc.* or by the sign, ◁. *Decrescendo, diminuendo,* and *morendo* are all words for decreasing loudness, as is the sign, ▷ .

7. The slur looks like a tie except that it connects two or more notes of different pitch. Slurred notes are played smoothly joined together.

8. A phrase mark looks like a very long slur, longer than a measure; it shows the unity of a musical idea. It does not necessarily mean that all the notes under it are smoothly joined, just that they belong in one "breath."

9. Tempo is indicated usually just at the beginning of a piece, generally with an Italian word such as *allegro* (fast), *adagio* (slow), etc. Sometimes composers add the more precise metronome mark, such as ♩ = 60, which would mean 60 quarter notes to the minute.

10. Expressive indications written into music are usually written in Italian, which has long been, by common consent, the international language for musical notation.

VII. INTERVALS

Naming intervals

The difference in pitch between two notes is referred to as an *interval*. If the two notes are played at the same time the interval is a *harmonic interval*, and if they are played one after the other the proper term is *melodic interval*.

The intervals are named according to the number of scale notes they include. That's equivalent to saying that they are named for the number of staff lines and spaces they include, or the number of letter names. For instance, the interval from C to G covers five lines and spaces or five letters: C (D, E, F,) G, so it is called a *fifth*. E to F covers only two letters, so it's a *second*. Similarly, D to F is a *third*: D, (E), F. D to F# is also a third, but a different kind. Here are some examples of the basic intervals in harmonic form:

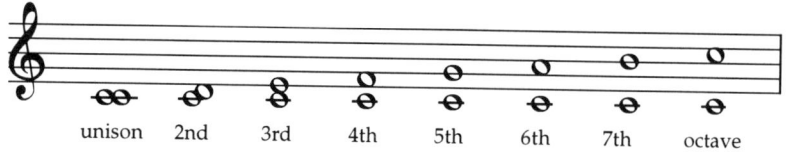

| unison | 2nd | 3rd | 4th | 5th | 6th | 7th | octave |

Figure 1: Some harmonic intervals formed with C

Each type of interval can have different *qualities*, which are determined by counting halfsteps. A third whose quality is *major*, such as C-E, is a halfstep larger than a *minor third* like D-F. A major third includes 4 halfsteps, while a minor third has only 3 halfsteps.

There are further qualities beyond major and minor: an interval can sometimes be larger than major or smaller than minor. For example, F to A# is a third that has five halfsteps, one halfstep larger than major.

If an interval is a halfstep larger than major it is called *augmented,* and if it is a halfstep smaller than minor it is called *diminished.* Augmented and diminished intervals are often identified with the signs "+ "and "°."

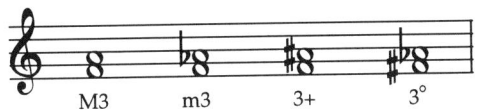

Figure 2: Four different kinds of thirds

Unisons, fifths, fourths, and *octaves* cannot be called major or minor; they have one basic quality: *perfect.* A *perfect fifth,* for example, has seven halfsteps; a perfect fourth has five halfsteps. But like the major-minor intervals, the quality of a perfect interval can also be altered by changing the number of halfsteps it contains. If a unison, fifth, fourth or octave is a halfstep larger than perfect it is augmented; if it is a halfstep smaller than perfect it is diminished. For example, B to F (going upward) is spelled as a fifth, B (C, D, E,) F, but it has only six halfsteps, so it is a *diminished fifth.*

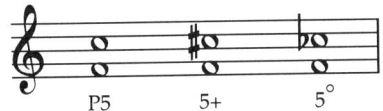

Figure 3: Three different kinds of fifth

To identify an interval correctly you must do two things: first get the numeric name of the interval by counting the number of letter names it covers, and then count the half steps in it to determine its quality.

 21

Activity

When you first start Practica Musica it is in "practice mode." In practice mode Practica Musica will identify any intervals or chords that you play on the screen keyboard or on an external MIDI keyboard. You can use this analysis capability to begin to familiarize yourself with interval names. Click the mouse on middle C, which is the C marked with a small indicator in the keyboard frame. You'll see the note "middle C"

(cont'd)

appear in staff notation and you'll hear it played. Now click on various other white keys (just the white keys at first) and watch what Practica Musica says about the intervals formed with middle C. Be sure to play the interval each time by clicking the "play selected notes" button. After hearing the interval and seeing it identified, turn off the note by clicking on it again and try a different note, leaving the starting note of middle C as it is (if you're still unsure of the lettername for each key, select the "staff keyboard" from the Options menu). Can you now begin to predict how Practica Musica will identify what you play? Would you be be able to identify the interval yourself? You could play this game with a friend or just by yourself: pick out a white key to combine with middle C and try to tell in advance what Practica Musica will call the interval when you play it. Remember to use just white keys for now, to avoid the extra problem of paying attention to flats and sharps. Practica Musica is always correct in these identifications, so it can settle any disputes.

Beyond augmented and diminished

In theory, intervals can even be *doubly* or *triply* augmented or diminished but you won't often see such oddities (if you want to experiment, start up Practica Musica and enter the notes Ab and D# on the staff — can you guess what this interval would be called?).

Identifying intervals quickly

One aid to interval identification is to memorize the qualities of the "natural intervals," which are the intervals as they appear in the C major scale, with no sharps or flats. Then you can use them as standards with which to compare intervals that do have sharps or flats.

All natural fifths or fourths on the staff are perfect except those between B and F, for example. So if you see a non-natural fifth like C— G# you remember that the natural fifth C—G is perfect, and since this one's upper note is raised a half step it must be one halfstep larger than perfect. So C—G# is an *augmented fifth.*

Similarly, all natural thirds are either major or minor:

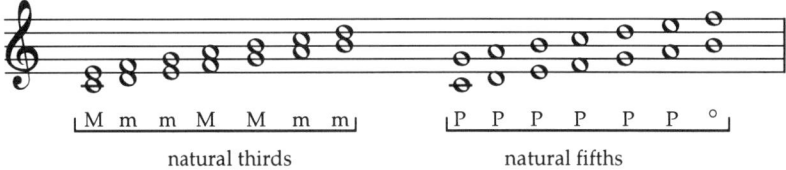

Figure 4: Qualities of the natural intervals

It is very important to memorize the qualities of the natural thirds and fifths . When you see B ascending to D you will know instantly that B-D is a minor third, containing 3 halfsteps. So if you encounter instead a Bb—D you'll know that since the B is now lowered a halfstep the interval has gotten larger than its natural version and therefore it must be a major third.

Even more simple is the case of an interval that is just like a natural one except that both of its notes have been raised or lowered by the same amount. This, of course, has no effect on the name of the interval, which remains the same in both numeric size and quality:

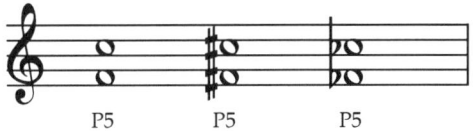

Figure 5: Perfect fifths on F, F#, and Fb

Knowing the qualities of the natural thirds and the natural fifths/fourths will also help you to quickly determine the qualities of other intervals. For example, a sixth can be regarded as a perfect fourth added to a third (note that this isn't quite like arithmetic — in musical intervals 4 + 3 equals 6!). *Adding a perfect interval never changes the quality of the result,*

so if the sixth looks like a minor third plus a perfect fourth then the sixth
itself must be minor, too:

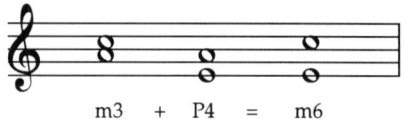

$$m3 \quad + \quad P4 \quad = \quad m6$$

Figure 6: Minor plus perfect equals minor

Similarly, a seventh could be seen as a third added to a perfect
fifth. So a major third on top of a perfect fifth must add up to a major
seventh:

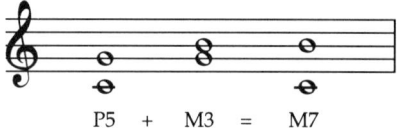

$$P5 \quad + \quad M3 \quad = \quad M7$$

Figure 7: Major plus perfect equals major

Finally, if you want to adopt the brute-force method of calcula-
tion you can just count the halfsteps in the interval, look at its spelling (the
number of letter names it includes) and consult a chart like the one below.
This chart lists the interval types and the number of halfsteps each
contains. The abbreviations are P = perfect, m = minor, M = major, ° =
diminished, + = augmented, "U" = unison, "O"= octave. Notice that two
possible answers are given for each size in halfsteps. An augmented
second and a minor third, for example, both have 3 halfsteps.

Number of halfsteps in interval

0	1	2	3	4	5	6	7	8	9	10	11	12
PU or 2°	U+ or m2	M2 or 3°	2+ or m3	M3 or 4°	3+ or P4	4+ or 5°	P5 or 6°	m6 or 5+	M6 or 7°	6+ or m7	M7 or O°	7+ or PO

Abbreviated name of interval, considering only those most likely to be encountered.

Figure 8: Chart of the intervals.

22

Activity

Now that you've had a little practice in identifying intervals it's time to try writing them out on request. That is an even better way to make sure that you understand how they are named.

Select Interval Spelling from your Practica Musica Activities menu, and then select Level 1 from the Interval Spelling menu. Practica Musica will ask you to play or write a certain interval on the screen. You have as much time to do this as you wish, and you can change your answer and even listen to it until you think it is correct. When you're ready, click "Evaluate" and Practica Musica will analyze what you have done and put the result at the top of the screen. If correct, you get a point. If incorrect, your score will be cut in half (!) and Practica Musica will both correct your answer and tell you what it was that you actually wrote. This is a game, of course, which is why your score can so easily be reduced. Be very careful with your answer if your score is close to the top!

Inverting intervals

If you reverse the notes of an interval you obtain its *inversion*. For example, C rising to E is a major third; its inversion is E rising to C, a minor sixth. Knowing the principle of inversion is handy for quick recognition, because *inversion reverses an interval's quality*. Major intervals become minor upon inversion; diminished intervals become augmented. Perfect intervals, however, remain perfect. As for the number of the interval, it is always 9 minus the old number: a sixth, for example, will invert to a third (9 minus 6 equals 3).

So if you see the note C with a B above it, you can use the inversion principle to quickly identify the interval as a major seventh: if the B were below the C it would be a minor second away (that's easier to count out than a seventh), and a minor second inverts to a major seventh (minor inverts to major; 9 minus 2 equals 7).

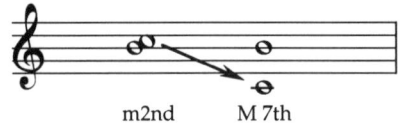

m2nd   M 7th

Figure 9: Using inversion to identify a seventh

23

Activity

With Practica Musica in practice mode (as it appears before beginning an activity) turn on any note by clicking the mouse on the keyboard. Then click on any note that is above the note you started with. Notice the name of the interval as identified by Practica Musica. Now turn off that second note and turn on the note of the same name *below* your starting note (you can use the "staff keyboard" to help you identify the note of the same name). The resulting interval will be the inversion of the one you started with. For example: With A as the starting note we turn on the D above it. That makes a "perfect fourth." Then we turn off that high D and try the D below the A. That produces a "perfect fifth," the inversion of a perfect fourth:

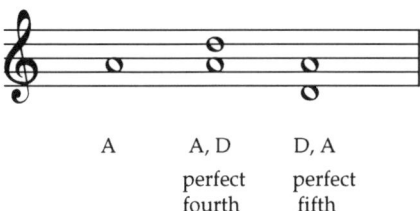

A   A, D   D, A

           perfect   perfect
           fourth   fifth

Try doing this exercise until you can reliably predict what the name of the inverted interval will be.

More about enharmonic equivalents

The most common mistake in identifying or writing intervals is to confuse *enharmonic equivalents* such as F# and Gb or E and Fb (*enharmonic equivalents* are notes or intervals or chords that are spelled differently and yet use the same keys on a piano).

A *second*, the difference between any two adjacent scale steps, will always be spelled with two adjacent letter names. F to Gb is a second, as are F to G and F to G#. However, F to F# is not a second but a kind of *unison*, since it involves only one letter name — even though the F# is played on the same piano key as the Gb.

What matters for naming an interval is not how it sounds, but how it is written on the staff.

Similarly, a *third* such as C to E is not at all the same thing as C to Fb, though the two use the same piano keys and have the same number of halfsteps. C to Fb would actually be called a kind of *fourth* — in this case a *diminished fourth* — because it includes four letter names: C, D, E, F, and yet has one halfstep less than an ordinary *perfect* fourth like C—F.

Figure 10: A pair of enharmonic intervals

This distinction is not just a matter of being fussy about technicalities. The choice of name for a note can provide information about that note's role in the music: in some circumstances, for example, "F#" could imply that a note is on its way upward to G, while "Gb" might mean that the direction is downward to F. Most importantly, the use of the correct name has important implications for understanding *harmony*, which will be the subject of later chapters.

24

Activity

The slight difference in pitch that distinguishes enharmonically equivalent notes has been lost on the modern piano but is often observed by musicians playing more flexible instruments. Practica Musica can demonstrate this traditional difference in pitch between enharmonic equivalents. With the program again in practice mode (not in any particular activity) select the "enharmonic keyboard" from the Options menu. Turn off MIDI if you are using it, and select one of the built-in Practica Musica instruments on the right side of the screen keyboard. Now turn on the Melody Button at the bottom left of the screen keyboard and use the Temperament option to select "extended meantone."

Slide the mouse from F# to Gb, or from E# to F. Do you notice the difference in pitch between these enharmonic equivalents? Now change the tuning back to equal temperament (the modern standard) and try the same comparison again. The equal temperament makes equivalent sharps and flats sound the same, for sake of convenience, but in earlier times different tunings were used in which the key between F and G, for example, could be used for F# but not for Gb. There are musical advantages to both the old and the new systems.

Compound intervals

If you add an octave to an interval it retains its basic character. Such intervals are known as *compound intervals*:

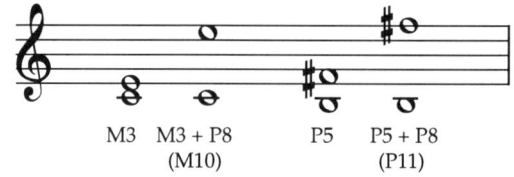

M3   M3 + P8   P5   P5 + P8
        (M10)   (P11)

Figure 11: Simple and compound versions of two intervals

Sometimes specific names are used for these: a third plus an octave can be called a *tenth*, a fourth plus an octave an *eleventh*, a fifth plus an octave a *twelfth*, and so on.

Consonance and dissonance

One of the most misunderstood concepts in all of music is that of *dissonance*. Dissonance is the name given to the quality of "disagreement" or "instability" that we may perceive between two or more simultaneous notes; it contrasts the feeling of *consonance* that we notice in other cases. We say, for example, that a *second* is dissonant, but a *fifth* is consonant:

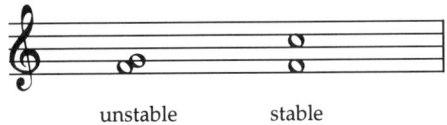

unstable   stable

Figure 12: A dissonant second and a consonant perfect fifth

All that is meant by this distinction is that one interval has a greater sense of stability than the other. You will sometimes hear dissonance defined as an "unpleasant" quality, but most musicians would argue that, on the contrary, dissonance is quite enjoyable if it is properly handled. Dissonance has always been the delight of composers, whose work would be static and empty without it, and many of our favorite moments in music depend on a dissonant effect. But in *tonal music of the style we are studying* — that is, music based on major and minor scales and using chords in the manner we'll discuss later — it is essential that dissonances be treated carefully: usually they will need to be followed quickly by a contrasting consonant interval as part of what is called *resolution* of the dissonance. For now let's just determine which intervals are considered consonant and which are dissonant.

The stable or consonant intervals are the unison, the octave, the fifth, third, and sixth:

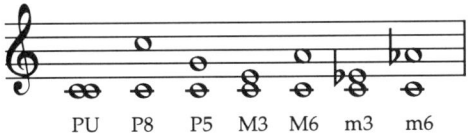

PU   P8   P5   M3   M6   m3   m6

Figure 13: The consonant intervals with C as bass

All other intervals are unstable or dissonant: the second, seventh, and every augmented or diminished interval, especially the
augmented fourth and diminished fifth:

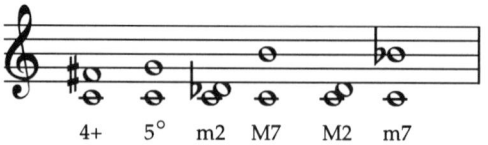

          4+   5°   m2   M7   M2   m7

Figure 14: The dissonant intervals with C as bass

The perfect fourth is special: in classical tonal music it's treated
as dissonant only if one of its notes is the bass, or lowest note sounding.
If it's in the upper voices as part of a chord then it's treated as consonant:

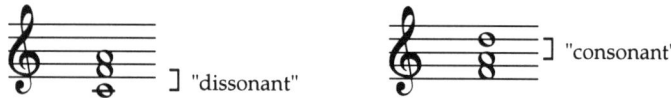

Figure 15: The dissonant perfect fourth and the consonant perfect fourth

When we reach the topic of harmony you'll see how dissonance
is used to give movement and drama to music.

25

Activity

You have now become familiar with the names of the various
intervals and how to spell them in staff notation. The next step is to learn
to recognize them by ear.

Select Interval Ear Training from your Practica Musica Activities
menu and then select Level 1 from the Interval Ear Training menu. You'll
be asked to identify an interval by name and also to find its second note

(cont'd)

on the keyboard. It doesn't matter whether you identify it first or locate it on the keyboard first; once you have done both the program will go on to another example. If Practica Musica notices that you have gained sufficient skill in distinguishing certain intervals it will proceed to others.

Graduating through all four levels of Interval Ear Training may take quite a bit of effort if you have not had much experience with music. Have faith, however: you can do it if you keep trying and listen carefully (you can play each interval as many times as you wish without penalty). The existence of "tin ears" has not been proven! Most people who think they are hopeless in this regard can eventually learn to hear intervals well.

SUPPLEMENTARY TOPICS, CHAPTER VII

Enharmonic dissonances

Some readers may have noticed that certain dissonances are identical in sound, at least on a piano, with some of the consonances. For example, the augmented second and minor third sound the same on a piano; they are *enharmonic*, yet one is classed as dissonant while the other is consonant. Just remember that their "dissonance" is partly a matter of what they traditionally imply harmonically, and also that on some instruments the two can in fact sound different. In tonal music a dissonant spelling can indicate that the interval in question is not stable but rather is unsettled and about to change; the dissonant note could then be called a *tendency tone* that implies movement. To the eyes of a musician, the second note of a melodic augmented second is probably moving upward and may benefit from some stretching in that direction if it is being played on an instrument that allows flexibility of pitch. A minor third, on the other hand, is more stable and has no such tendency. The significance of correctly-spelled dissonances will become more apparent when we reach the topic of chords.

Summary, Chapter VII

1. Two notes of different pitch form an *interval*. If the notes are played at the same time we call it a *harmonic interval*; otherwise it's a *melodic interval*.

2. Intervals are named according to the number of letter names they include. C to G#, for instance, covers five letters, C, D, E, F, G, so it is a kind of *fifth*. Other intervals are the *unison, second, third, fourth, sixth, seventh, and octave*.

3. The second, third, sixth, and seventh have two basic qualities, called *major* and *minor*. Beyond that they can also be augmented or diminished. C to Eb is a *minor third*; C to E is a *major third*, C to Ebb is a *diminished third* and C to E# is an *augmented third*.

4. The unison, octave, fifth and fourth have one basic quality, called *perfect*. Beyond that they can be enlarged one half-step to make them *augmented* or reduced one half-step to make them *diminished*. From C to G# is an *augmented fifth*. C to Gb is a *diminished fifth*.

5. If the order of notes in an interval is reversed, you obtain its *inversion*. The number of an inverted interval is always 9 minus the number of the uninverted interval, and the *quality* (major-minor, diminished-augmented) of an interval reverses when it is inverted. Example: the M3 C-E inverts to the m6 E-C.

6. Intervals that use the same keys on the piano but are spelled differently, such as the augmented third C-E# and the perfect fourth C-F, are known as *enharmonic equivalents*. They have different musical meanings and functions despite their practical effect on the piano.

7. *Consonance* refers to the feeling of stability produced by certain intervals such as the unison, octave, fifth, third, and sixth. *Dissonance* is the instability associated with intervals such as the second, seventh, or augmented fourth or diminished fifth. In classical tonal music the perfect fourth is considered dissonant when one of its notes is the bass, or current lowest note in the harmony.

VIII. MORE SCALES

The harmonic minor

One of the most common reasons for using an accidental in a melody is to make use of an alternate form of the minor scale. The natural minor, as we have seen, uses only the notes designated by the key signature, but there are other minor scales. For example, composers often want to raise the seventh note of a minor scale to make it lead back to the tonic — in other words, they want to give it a *leading tone* such as the major scale has: a seventh note that is only one halfstep away from the tonic. To accomplish this, the seventh degree of the natural minor must be raised with an accidental of some sort, forming what we call the *harmonic minor* (when we get to chords you'll see why it's called that). For example:

G natural minor   G harmonic minor

Figure 1: Raising the seventh degree to make the harmonic minor

The harmonic form of the minor requires no changes in the key signature. The seventh degree is always raised by writing in a special sharp or natural. Note also that when we alter a scale tone we *never change its letter name.* F becomes F#, not Gb.

The melodic minor

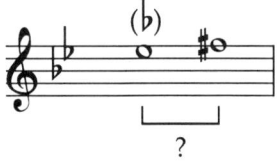

Figure 2.

Now that you can identify intervals you'll be able to see that the harmonic minor scale has an unusual feature. What would you call the interval between its sixth and seventh degrees (Figure 2) ?

Correct. This interval, the *augmented second*, was long regarded as awkward or at least exotic. When composers wanted to avoid the augmented second but still intended to use the raised seventh degree they raised the sixth degree as well, making the interval between the two an ordinary major second. Because the goal of this alteration was to produce smoother melody we call this form of minor the *melodic minor*:

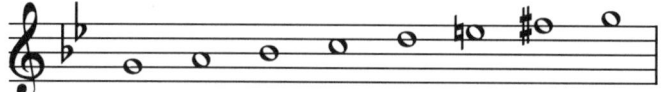

Figure 3: Forming the melodic minor with a natural

Notice that we raised the sixth degree by using a natural sign on what would otherwise have been an Eb. In other scales it might be necessary to use a sharp to get the same result, as in melodic A minor:

Figure 4: Forming the melodic minor with a sharp

You'll often see the melodic minor written in textbooks with two forms: one for going up and one for coming down:

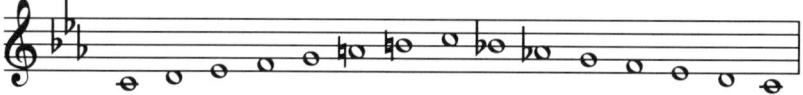

Figure 5: C melodic minor as often seen in textbooks

In practice there is often no real need to define the melodic minor as having different forms for ascent and descent, because all three forms of the minor may be mixed up in a single piece. The "descending melodic minor" is really just the natural minor again. On the other hand, the textbook definition of melodic minor gives us a handy way to describe tunes such as the Scottish folk song "Charlie is my darling," whose character is based on its use of both raised and natural sixth and seventh degrees:

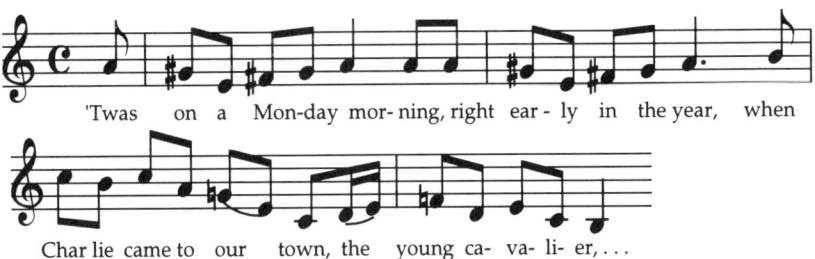

 Figure 6: From the Scottish folk song, "Charlie is my Darling"
(available for listening)

The raised 6th and 7th degrees are the F# and G#, which revert to naturals in the second line when the melodic direction is mostly downward.

The pentatonic scale

The pentatonic scale is found in the folk music of many peoples as well as in composed music. Almost anything you play in the pentatonic scale sounds melodious because there's no way to make a dissonant leap (it contains no augmented fourth or diminished fifth). It is built in this pattern: whole step, whole step, minor third, whole step — just like the black keys of the piano, or like a major scale without the fourth and seventh degrees. If you play a melody using only black keys you are playing in a pentatonic scale.

"Amazing Grace" is a good example of a pentatonic melody:

Figure 7: A pentatonic melody (available for listening)

The only notes in "Amazing Grace" are F, G, A, C, and D.

"Come all you fair and tender maidens" is a different sort of pentatonic melody. Though it uses the same five notes as "Amazing Grace" it gives a minor effect by emphasizing the "D" and the minor third above it:

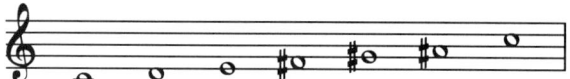
Figure 8 : Another pentatonic melody (available for listening)

The wholetone scale

As the name suggests, the wholetone scale is composed entirely of whole steps. A non-traditional scale, it has no dominant and therefore you can't make any of its notes sound like a "tonic," which gives wholetone music a sense of being adrift without a compass.

Figure 9: A wholetone scale on C

Claude Debussy often used the wholetone scale:

Figure 10. Wholetones in Debussy's *Prélude à "L'après-midi d'un faune"*

26

Activity

Select Scales from your Practica Musica Activities menu and try Level 3. In this level you'll be asked to play various of the above scales, and Practica Musica will help you find the notes. If you graduate from Level 3 that will show that you understand all the scales presented so far and also that you have some familiarity with the keyboard.

SUPPLEMENTARY TOPICS, CHAPTER VIII

The modes

The major and minor scales are the survivors of a number of scales or *modes* that date from medieval times. The modes are still occasionally heard today, especially in folk music and jazz. You can get something of an idea of the flavor of the modes if you play just the white keys using D, E, F, or G as a tonic. The mode starting on D is known as the *Dorian* mode; E is the tonic for the *Phrygian;* F for the *Lydian,* and G for the *MixoLydian.* The major and natural minor scales are sometimes called the *Ionian* and the *Aeolian* modes.

Practica Musica is able to invent melodies using the notes of the medieval modes (see the Choose Scale button in the Custom level of Pitch Dictation, for example) although its tunes are not in the medieval style or even, strictly speaking, really modal. Remember that if you want to write a modal melody yourself it is important to emphasize its tonic and perhaps its dominant — just as you need to do when distinguishing "A minor" from "C major ." You can emphasize the tonic and dominant degrees by thinking of them as melodic destinations or stopping points. Phrases or sections will usually end on either the dominant or the tonic.

The Dorian mode is probably the most familiar to our ears. The only difference between Dorian and natural minor is the sixth degree, which is a halfstep higher in Dorian. The asterisk marks the occurence of that sixth degree in this well-known traditional song:

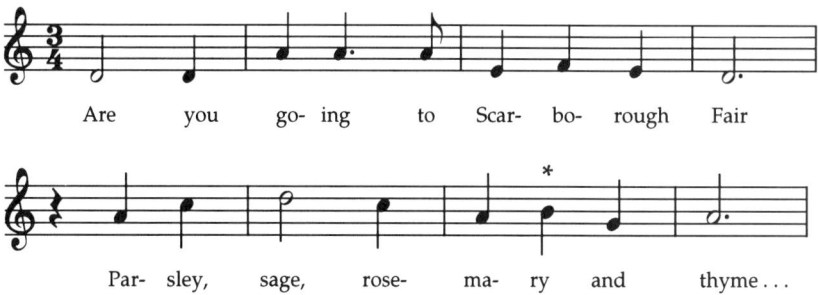

 Figure 11: A tune in the Dorian mode (available for listening)

The chromatic scale

If you write a scale that is all halfsteps you'll find that you need to include some *chromatic* halfsteps, halfsteps in which the lettername does not change, such as F to F#. That is why a scale made of all halfsteps is often called the *chromatic scale*. The other scales we have been studying use only *diatonic* halfsteps in which the lettername changes, such as E to F or G# to A, and for that reason the other scales are called *diatonic scales*.

The spelling of the halfsteps in a chromatic scale is variable, except that B-C and E-F are almost always spelled diatonically. The below arrangement is one possibility:

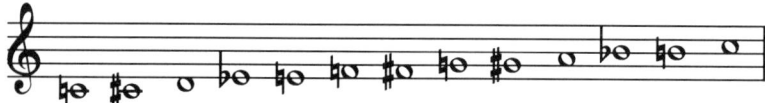

Figure 12: A chromatic scale starting on C

Summary, Chapter VIII

1. *The harmonic minor* scale is the same as the natural minor except that the seventh degree is raised one half-step to provide a leading tone back to the tonic. The raising is always accomplished by use of accidentals; it is not indicated in the key signature.

2. The *melodic minor* scale is the same as the harmonic minor except that the sixth degree is also raised, to eliminate the augmented second found between the sixth and seventh degrees of the harmonic minor. The melodic minor is usually represented as reverting to natural minor when it is descending, though in practice this is not always true.

3. The *pentatonic* scale is used extensively in folk music all over the world. It has five notes, which are arranged like the black keys of a piano: wholestep, wholestep, minor third, wholestep. It is like a major scale without the fourth and seventh degrees.

4. The *wholetone* scale is composed entirely from wholesteps. It has only six notes and does not have a clear tonic.

Supplementary Topics

5. The medieval *modes* are predecessors of our modern major and minor scales. The pattern of steps for each mode can be found in the white keys of the piano: the mode beginning on D is the *Dorian*, E is the tonic for the *Phrygian*, F for the *Lydian*, and G for the *Mixolydian*. Our major and natural minor scales are sometimes called the *Ionian* and *Aeolian* modes.

6. The *chromatic scale* is composed all of half-steps. It gets its name from the fact that some of these must necessarily be *chromatic half-steps*, half-steps in which both notes have the same letter name, such as C to C#. A *diatonic* halfstep is one in which the lettername changes, such as E-F or G#-A. The major and minor scales and the modes are called *diatonic scales* for this reason: they include only diatonic halfsteps.

IX. TRIADS

The origins of triadic harmony

Now that you understand consonance and dissonance and how to classify intervals it's possible to discuss *harmony*. Harmony is the art of combining simultaneous pitches. We'll use the term *chord* to refer to a combination of three or more different pitch classes, and keep the term *interval* for combinations of only two pitch classes.

The type of harmony we are studying, the harmony that forms the basis of classical music and most popular music, is called *tonal harmony*. It is based on a particular kind of chord called the *triad*. A triad is formed by combining the intervals of the fifth and the third; in its simplest form it looks like two thirds stacked together:

Figure 1: A triad on C

Triads arise naturally whenever you try to make several different musical parts all consonant with each other. In fact, *a major or minor triad* (see below) *is the only possible group of three notes in which all are different pitch classes and all are consonant with each other*; that is why the triad has come to have such importance in tonal harmony. Tonal harmony depends on the resolution of dissonance by consonance, and triads provide that resolution.

The major and minor triads

Consonant triads are composed of a major third and a minor third, which add up to a perfect fifth. If the major third is the lower of the two the triad is called a *major triad,* and if the minor third is in the lower position then the triad is a *minor triad*:

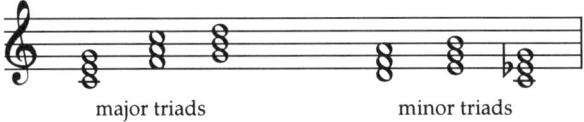

major triads   minor triads

Figure 2: major and minor triads

Parts of a triad

The note that the triad is built on is called its *root.* The triad's middle note is its *third*, a third above the root, and its upper note is its *fifth*, a fifth above the root. In the above examples the roots of the major triads are C, F, and G, and the roots of the minor triads are D, E, and C. Triads are identified by their roots and by their quality, so the first three of the above examples could be called C major, F major, and G major triads. The last three would be D minor, E minor, and C minor triads.

 27

Activity

With Practica Musica in practice mode (not in any activity) try building some triads on various notes of the C major scale. Practica Musica will identify the name and quality of each chord as you write it, and you can hear each chord by clicking the "play selected notes" button.

To play several notes simultaneously you'll need first to click the "harmony" button, which is at the lower left side of the keyboard. Once that is done, just click on the staff where you want the note to be, or click on one of the keys of the screen piano. If you have a MIDI keyboard, just play the notes on that. You can turn a note off by clicking on it again, or by pressing the spacebar to clear all current notes. MIDI notes will turn off when you release the keys on the MIDI instrument.

(cont'd)

Start by entering the note C. Then add E, noticing that the program tells you this is a major third. Add G to complete the C major triad and then play it. The analysis line will identify this chord: "major triad, root is C." Now click on the E key to turn it off and put in Eb instead. How is this chord identified? Play the chord to hear the difference.

Try building a triad on each of the notes of the C major scale, using only the white keys. Play each one and observe how it is identified by Practica Musica, and then try changing its quality by sharping or flatting the third (middle note) of the triad. If the triad is minor, make it major; if it is major, make it minor.

What happens with the triad built on B? The program will identify this as a *diminished* triad. Do you notice that it does not sound "finished" as the major and minor triads do? Can you guess why? How could you alter this chord to make it sound finished? (hint: you need to sharp one of the upper notes).

Dissonant chords

The triad B D F is said to be *diminished* because its fifth is diminished rather than being perfect like the fifths of the major and minor triads. The diminished triad consists of two minor thirds. To label a diminished triad we use lowercase numerals, since it is based on minor thirds, and we add the symbol "°" to indicate the diminished quality.

The diminished fifth is a dissonant, unstable interval, and so the diminished triad is also dissonant: because of its unstable nature it doesn't work well as a conclusion or as a point of rest; it doesn't sound "finished."

You can also make an *augmented triad*, though it is not used very often. The augmented triad is composed of two major thirds, which together form an augmented fifth. The augmented fifth sounds like a minor sixth on a piano, but it is technically dissonant (remember that "dissonance" refers to musical instability, not to unpleasantness). The chord would be labeled in uppercase numerals with a "+" to show the augmentation.

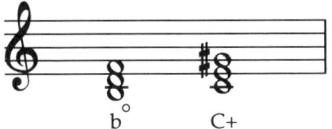

Figure 3: A diminished triad and an augmented triad

Naming the natural triads of a key

There are only seven triads that can be made from the notes of a single major or natural minor scale. These seven define the harmonic world for that *key*, and they are often identified by the Roman numeral of their root. For instance, the triad built on the first note of a major scale is called I, the triad built on the fourth note is called IV, and so on. If the chord is minor a lowercase Roman numeral is used: the chord on the sixth note of a major scale is the minor triad vi. The key of C major is defined by these seven chords, which use only the notes of the C major scale:

Figure 4: Building triads on each scale degree

The primary triads

As you can see from the uppercase Roman numerals, only three of these chords are major: the ones built on I, IV, and V. Also called the *tonic, subdominant,* and *dominant triads,* they are the most important chords in tonal music. Many folk and pop songs use only I, IV, and V, and even many of the best-known classical themes are based on them alone. We call these three the *primary triads*:

Figure 5: The primary triads for the key of C major

The secondary triads

The remaining triads of the key, the ones built on the second, third, sixth, and seventh degrees, provide variety and complexity. We call them the *secondary triads*:

Figure 6: The secondary triads for the key of C major

No matter what major key you are using, the primary and secondary triads always have the same qualities. As long as you use only the notes natural to the key, which means the notes defined by the key signature, then the I, IV, and V triads will always be major, the ii, iii, and vi triads will always be minor, and the vii chord will always be diminished.

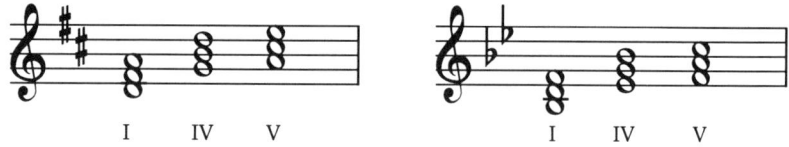

Figure 7: Primary triads for the keys of D major and Bb major

28

Activity

Select Chord Playing or Chord Spelling from your Practica Musica Activities menu and begin Level 1. Chord Playing is the best choice for beginners because Practica Musica will supply the correct "enharmonics" for you (that is, if you click on the right piano key the program will decide whether it should be called, for example, F# or Gb). In Chord Spelling you'll need to choose the enharmonics yourself.

(cont'd)

Like most of the Practica Musica activities, Chord Playing is a game in which you try to gain a score high enough to "graduate" from the level. You'll be asked questions such as "please play an F major triad," and you should respond by playing the keys that correspond to an F major triad (you can also place the notes directly on the staff, using the mouse). You can listen to the notes you have entered and change them as needed until you think you've got it right. Then click on "my answer is ready" and Practica Musica will evaluate your answer, awarding you a point if it was correct and cutting your current score in half if it was not. It will also identify the chord you have entered and if the chord was incorrect it will tell you what was wrong and will print a corrected chord just to the right of your answer. When you make mistakes be sure to look at the corrected answer to see what you should have entered! And don't worry too much about the score: Practica Musica will not save your score to disk unless it is better than your previous efforts.

Changes in the minor keys

If you build triads on each degree of a natural minor scale, again using only the notes of the scale, the quality of each chord will of course be different from what it was in the major keys. The tonic, subdominant, and dominant triads, for example, will be minor instead of major:

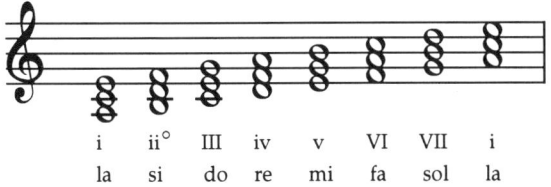

| i | ii° | III | iv | v | VI | VII | i |
| la | si | do | re | mi | fa | sol | la |

Figure 8: The triads natural to the key of A Minor

However, the dominant chord doesn't work very well if it's minor. The function of a dominant chord, as we'll see later, is to lead strongly back to the tonic, and for that it is necessary that the dominant chord contain the scale's *leading tone* — the note a half-step below the tonic. To provide the leading tone necessary for a strong dominant, composers usually raise the third of the minor dominant chord, making it major like the dominant in the major keys:

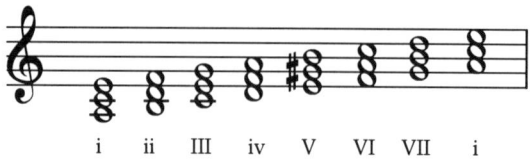

i   ii   III   iv   V   VI   VII   i

Figure 9: Altering the minor V chord to make it major

This is the origin of the *harmonic minor* scale: the alteration made to the dominant chord raises the seventh degree of the scale, allowing more effective harmony. This alteration is always accomplished with an accidental — not by adding to the key signature.

Sometimes what is needed is not a sharp but a natural, as follows:

Figure 10: Altering the V chord in C minor

When the seventh degree is raised it can affect other chords, too. The triad built on the raised seventh degree itself, vii$^\circ$, is often used as a substitute for the V chord, as in the major keys:

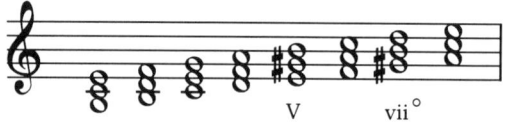

V   vii$^\circ$

Figure 11: The raised seventh will also be used to make vii$^\circ$ from VII.

The dominant seventh chord

The most important dissonant triad of all is made by adding one more third to the stack of two thirds that makes the dominant triad. This fourth note forms the interval of a seventh with the root, making a *seventh chord*. This particular seventh chord formed from the dominant triad is known as the *dominant seventh* (Figure 12).

The dominant seventh chord is particularly unstable because it contains not only a dissonant seventh but also a dissonant diminished fifth. It is usually used just before the tonic triad or the vi triad, either of which *resolves* that instability. The dominant seventh is labeled "V7," and is very common in all types of tonal music from classical to pop. It can, in fact be substituted for the plain V chord almost freely, and will give a stronger effect for the subsequent movement to the tonic chord. We'll discuss other dissonant chords later, but for now and for most common uses it will be sufficient to know just the V7 and the vii°. The vii°, itself a dissonant chord, is identical with the upper three notes of the dominant seventh chord, and is used in the same way as the V7.

To form the dominant seventh of any key just add a minor third on top of the dominant triad. In music written with a key signature you'll never need to add a flat or a sharp to the seventh, since it is always a scale note. For example, here are dominant seventh chords for several different keys:

Figure 12: Dominant seventh chords in several keys

Recognizing chords

If you are already familiar with written music you will know that it contains few chords that look exactly like the triads in the above examples. Triads seldom appear in such plain form; usually they are elaborated in some way. Some of their notes may be repeated or even omitted, and they may be arranged in a different order, with the root taking one of the upper positions instead of being the lowest note. And the chord can also be spread out horizontally, so that the notes are played one after another instead of all at the same time. We'll look in detail at each of these ways of elaborating chords.

Chord inversions

If the lowest note of a chord is the root, as in all the above examples, then we say that the chord is in *root position*.

If the triad's *third* is the bass, the chord is said to be in *first inversion*:

Figure 13: Triads in first inversion

Similarly, if we put the *fifth* in the bass the chord will be in *second inversion*:

Figure 14: Triads in second inversion

It's important to know that the arrangement of the upper voices doesn't affect the chord's inversion — any chord that has its third in the lowest position is in first inversion, regardless of how the other notes are distributed.

Inverted chords are often labeled with the numbers 6 or 6/4: a "IV 6" chord means a IV chord in first inversion; a "IV 6/4" would be a IV chord in second inversion. The numbers refer to intervals formed between the bass and the other notes: the first inversion chord includes a sixth above the bass and the second inversion includes both a sixth and a fourth (the numbers derive from the 17th-18th-century practice of *figured bass*, which is discussed in the Supplementary Topics section for this chapter).

The figured bass numbers should not be confused with a common practice in popular music where, for example, a C major triad with an "A" added to it is called a "C6" chord (since the A is a sixth above the C). Most often the figured bass numbers are used in connection with Roman numerals, as in IV 6; if you see a "6" after a letter name in a popular song book it will probably be referring to the "added sixth-chord" and not to a first inversion triad.

Doubling notes of a chord

If we decide to *double* (repeat) any of the notes of a chord the usual choice is to double the root. Next best is the fifth, and then the third.

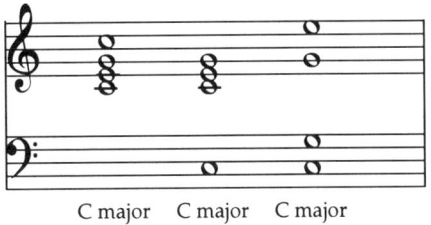

C major   C major   C major

Figure 15: Triads with doubled notes

Most chord examples later in this book will be written with four notes each (they'll be "four-voice" chords), and in most cases the root will be doubled.

It is also possible to leave out the fifth and still give the general impression of a triad, though it is incomplete. The root, of course, cannot be omitted without changing the nature of the chord, and the third is necessary to provide the chord's major or minor quality.

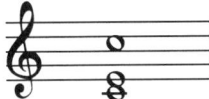

Figure 16: An incomplete triad with root doubled and fifth omitted

Voicing

You can vertically spread out the notes of a chord to let some "air" into it — this is called putting the chord into *open position*. On the other hand, when the notes are arranged so that all are as close to each other as possible the chord is said to be in *close position* ("close" as in the opposite of "far away.") So a chord of any inversion and with any kind of doubling can also be in either open or close position. In general, all these rearrangements of a chord that have no effect on its quality are called changes in *voicing*.

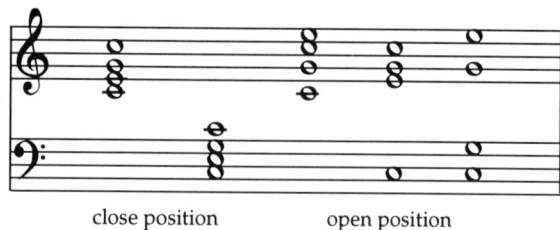

close position   open position

Figure 17: C major chords in open and close position

In piano and orchestra scoring it is common to voice chords so that the widest intervals are in the low notes and the upper notes make narrower intervals. In other words, the lower voices tend to be in open position and the upper voices in close position, as in this voicing of a C major triad:

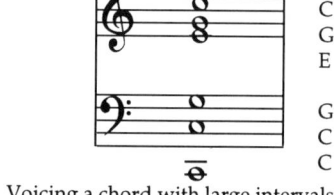

C
G
E

G
C
C

Figure 18: Voicing a chord with large intervals in the lower parts

29

Activity

With Practica Musica again in "practice harmony" mode, enter a C major triad and then place it in first inversion by turning off the low C and turning on a C above the other notes. The program will tell you what you have done; it should say "Major triad in first inversion, its root is C." Try converting this to a second inversion C major triad where G is the lowest note. Then double the root by adding another C and try rearranging the chord to an open voicing. You can experiment with various combinations of C, E, and G and use Practica Musica as a guide.

What happens if you write a close root position F major triad at the very bottom of the keyboard? Doesn't it sound "muddy?" That's because narrow intervals don't work very well at low pitches. Try voicing this way, counting upward: F F A C. Better? Notice that all four of the below examples are in root position; all that changes is the voicing.

(illustration on following page)

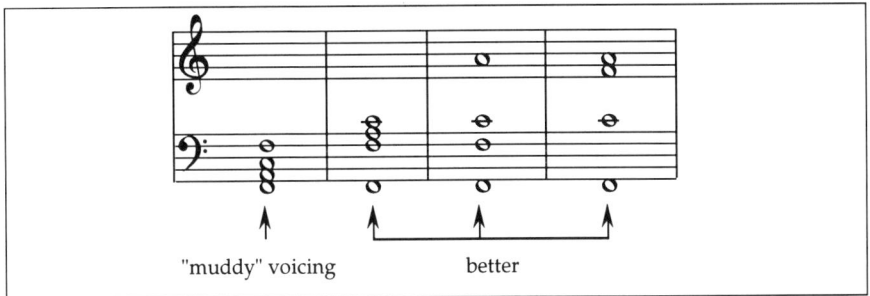

"muddy" voicing   better

30

Activity

Select the Chord Spelling activity and attempt to pass Level 2. In Level 2 you'll be asked to provide specific inversions of each chord. Again, Practica Musica will be able to show you the correct voicing if you make a mistake.

Broken or arpeggiated chords

The notes of a chord are often played one after another instead of all at once, which can make it harder to recognize on the page. Sometimes a melody will outline the notes of a particular chord, as in the opening of Beethoven's Third Symphony:

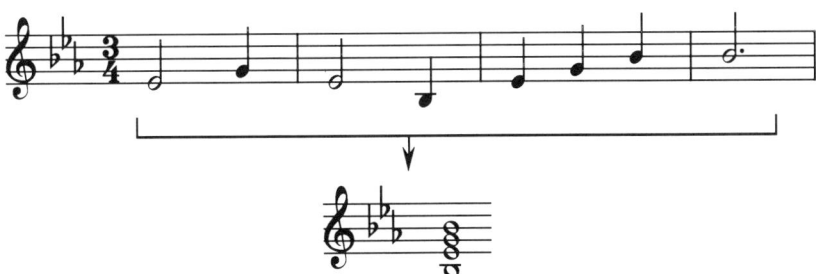

Figure 19: A triad outlined by notes of a melody

In piano music you will often see left-hand chords broken up in various patterns, a style called the *Alberti bass,* after the 18th-century composer who supposedly invented it:

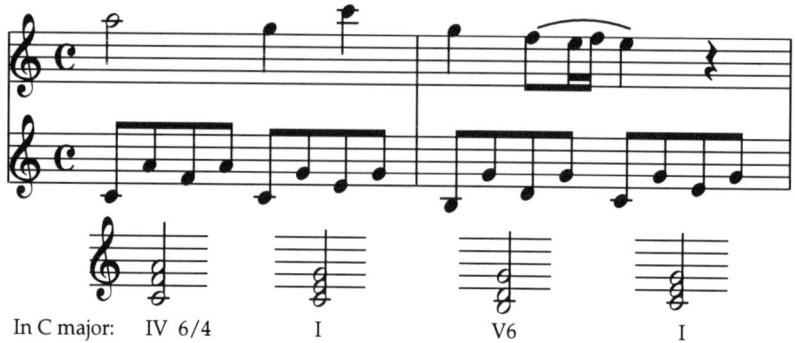

In C major: IV 6/4   I   V6   I

Figure 20: Alberti bass in Mozart's C Major Piano Sonata, K. 545
(available for listening in "Chapter 10, Figure 03")

The following measures illustrate several typical Alberti patterns:

Figure 21: Alberti patterns on a D major chord

The word *arpeggio* describes chord notes played one after another. It derives from the way harpists or guitarists sound a chord by drawing a finger across the strings:

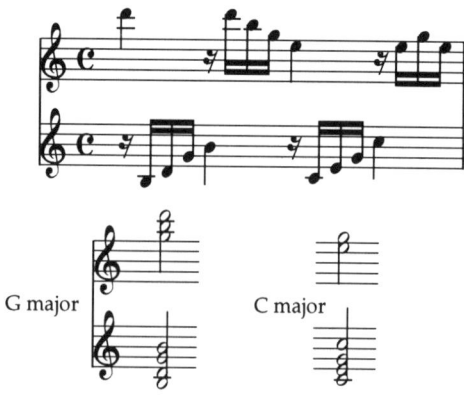

G major   C major

Figure 22: Arpeggiated chords from Mozart's C Major Sonata, K. 545

SUPPLEMENTARY TOPICS, CHAPTER IX

Figured bass (thoroughbass)

In the 17th and 18th centuries keyboard players often played from a sort of shorthand notation, much as a jazz artist might do today. What they had before them was a bass line — just the lowest notes of the accompaniment — with numbers underneath each note that indicated the required harmony. They improvised the rest, filling in chords and decorating them as they saw fit.

The bass line with numbers was called a *figured bass* or *thorough-bass*, and we still use its figures in labeling chords. Here's how it worked: each number appearing with the bass line was the number of an interval needed in the harmony, as measured from the bass note (but the intervals could be compound if desired, i.e., they could be increased by octaves). The designated chord could be played in any voicing or doubling:

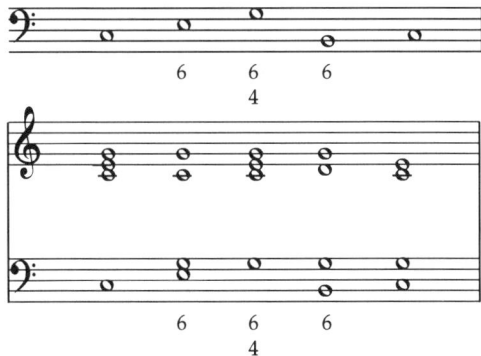

Figure 23: Figured bass, plain, then realized in simple chords

Translating the numbers into actual harmonies is called *realizing* the figured bass.

The figures were often abbreviated. A "5/3" (root position triad) was not usually written out because it is so common, so a bass note with no figure was assumed to be a "5/3." For the 6/3 (first inversion triad)

only the 6 was written. For the second inversion triad, however, both intervals were specified: 6/4. Today when referring to the various inversions of a triadic chord we use those abbreviated numbers:

"[no figure]" means "root position triad"
"6" means "first inversion triad"
"6/4" = "second inversion triad"

In addition, a flat or sharp prefixed to a number meant to use an accidental to alter the chord. A sharp or flat appearing alone in the figured bass without a number was assumed to be an abbreviation for a sharp third or flat third. So, for example, a composer using figured bass in a minor key could indicate a root position dominant chord altered to major simply by writing the root note with a "#" underneath it:

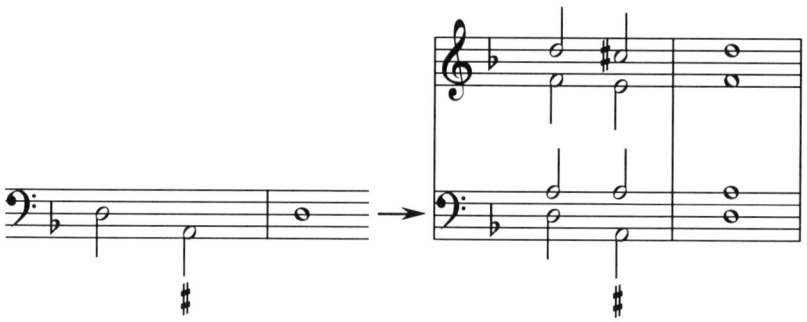

Figure 24: Realization of a short passage with raised third

Summary, Chapter IX

1. The *triad* is the basis of tonal harmony. The major and minor triads are the only chords whose notes are mutually consonant. A triad is built by stacking two thirds together; its outer notes are a fifth apart.

2. A *major triad* is a major third with a minor third on top; a *minor triad* is a minor third plus a major third. The other triads are dissonant: a *diminished triad* is two minor thirds and an *augmented triad* is two major thirds.

3. The notes of a triad may be rearranged in *inversions* without changing the basic nature of the chord. The original arrangement as two thirds stacked together is called *root* position. If the former middle note is placed in the bass that makes the *first inversion*; if the former top note is the bass then you have a *second inversion*. The order of the upper notes does not affect the inversion.

4. If you *double* (repeat) any of the notes of a triadic chord, the best one to double is the root. Next best is the fifth.

5. The fifth may sometimes be left out of a triadic chord, but the root and third are essential.

6. The chords of a given key are often referred to by the Roman numeral of the scale degree that they are built on (i.e., their root). Major or augmented chords are written with upper-case Roman numerals; minor or diminished chords receive the lower case. Diminished chords are further identified by the symbol " ° " and augmented ones by "+". The *primary triads* are the triads built on the tonic, dominant, and subdominant degrees of a major or minor scale. The *secondary triads* are all the others.

7. The primary and secondary triads have different qualities in a minor key: i, ii°, III, iv, v, VI, VII. The v is customarily converted to a major triad, V, so that it will move strongly to the tonic as it does in a major key. If the V is changed in this way the VII will also be changed to vii°. This alteration is accomplished with accidentals, not by changes in the key signature.

8. Adding one more natural third to the dominant triad creates the *dominant seventh chord* (V7) a dissonant chord that emphasizes the dominant's natural tendency to move to the tonic triad. The V7 can be freely substituted for the V chord when a stronger effect is needed.

9. Numbers borrowed from the old practice of figured bass are often used in identifying chord inversion. A "6" added to a Roman numeral means "first inversion triad." "6/4" means a second inversion triad. The numbers refer to the intervals that notes of the chord form with the bass note.

X. CHORD PROGRESSION

Principles of chord progression

When first discussing scales we mentioned that the tonic and the dominant have a very close relationship. Whether their affinity for each other is based on acoustic principles or on cultural traditions, or on both, is hard to say — but there is a certain magnetism between them. When you build triads on the tonic and dominant degrees of the scale the triads inherit that close relationship, giving a chord change from dominant to tonic a unique sense of logical resolution.

The energy possessed by the dominant-tonic chord change is at the heart of the technique that composers of tonal music use to propel a composition through a *progression* of harmonies. The technique rests both on the importance of the dominant-tonic relationship itself and on the capacity of other chord pairs to mimic that relationship.

The primary triads

If you were asked to describe the chord change from dominant to tonic in general terms you might list these features: the root of the second chord is a fourth above (or a fifth below) the root of the first one and the first chord is major (remember that even in a minor key we go to the trouble of altering the dominant to major). Both characteristics are illustrated in these four-voice examples:

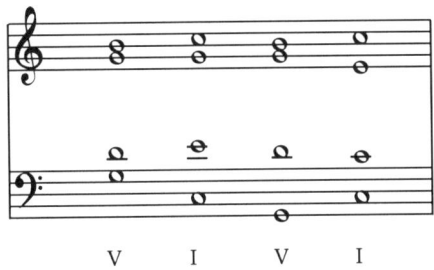

Figure 1: Root movement in the dominant-tonic change

There are other chord changes that have one or both of these characteristics, and which consequently have some of that same energy found in the dominant-tonic pair.

The most important of these other chord changes is that from the tonic to the subdominant (i.e., from the tonic triad to the triad built on the fourth note of a major or minor scale). This is because the tonic chord is in the same position relative to the subdominant as the dominant is in relative to the tonic — the only difference is that the movement is away from the tonic rather than toward it.

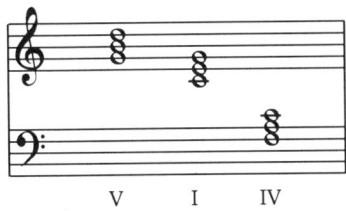

Figure 2: The relationship between I, IV, and V.

The I, IV, and V chords, then, share a unique and symmetrical relationship. These three, which we earlier called the *primary triads*, are the main connecting points of any progression — the big cities, so to speak, on your harmonic highway. For much of popular music and even many well-known classical themes these are the only chords you need to know.

The peculiar magic of the cycle between I, IV, and V is nowhere better illustrated than in the standard 12-measure blues progression, which works exactly the same way in hundreds of compositions.

The first line of a blues tune stays mostly on the tonic chord, with a side trip to the subdominant:

<pre>
        I   IV   I
Well I'm goin' away, baby, I won't be back 'till fall
</pre>

The second line (using the same text) begins with the subdominant and then returns to the tonic:

<pre>
        IV   I
Well I'm goin' away, baby, I won't be back 'till fall
</pre>

The third line finally reaches the dominant, which is usually a dominant seventh chord, and then delays return to the tonic by interjecting a subdominant again:

<pre>
        V7   IV   I
And if I find me a new love, I won't be back at all
</pre>

The cycle completes with a new dominant (after "I won't be back at all") which introduces a repeat of the whole thing — which can keep repeating for a long time. Because of the regular cycle of chord changes the musicians can make considerable innovations in melody and accompaniment without losing even inexperienced listeners.

The blues progression illustrates the tension between predictability and surprise that is at the heart of effective musical structures. A good chord progression cannot be entirely unpredictable; the listener wants some reassurance as well as surprise — or else there is no possibility of surprise! — and in tonal music that reassurance comes in such forms as the ultimate resolution of the dominant by the tonic.

Compare the blues progression to the beginning of Mozart's *Piano Sonata in C*:

Figure 3: From Mozart: *Sonata in C major*, K. 545 (available for listening)

This does sound different. But Mozart's piece is still based on the same logical interplay between the three strongest chords: tonic, subdominant, and dominant. Harmonically the two examples have much in common, at least in the first few measures.

Harmonic rhythm

You may have noticed that the chords in both the above examples change much less frequently than the notes do. This is true of most tonal music based on accompanied melody: we say that it tends to have *slow harmonic rhythm*. In most pieces the underlying chord, the one that "goes with" the melody, will change only once a measure or at the most, twice, unless the piece is very slow. Sometimes the chord won't change at all for several measures, as in the following example from Prokofiev's *Peter and the Wolf*:

Figure 4: From Prokofiev's "Peter and the Wolf"

J. S. Bach's famous *chorales*, short vocal works for four voices, are often studied for their harmony. The chorales could be said to have a fast harmonic rhythm, since they change chords on almost every beat:

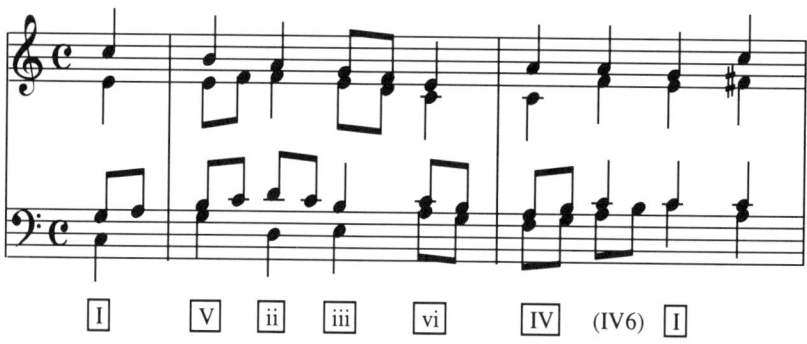

Figure 5: From a Bach chorale

Extending the dominant-tonic relationship

The idea that chords follow each other well if their roots are a fourth apart can be extended to the secondary triads. None of these changes has quite the strength of V-I or even I-IV, since they all begin with minor chords, but they still have a trace of that dominant-tonic relationship. For example, ii moves very nicely to V, iii to vi, and vi to ii. You can even string together a chain of such chords, as in this tune learned by every beginning piano student, "Heart and Soul:"

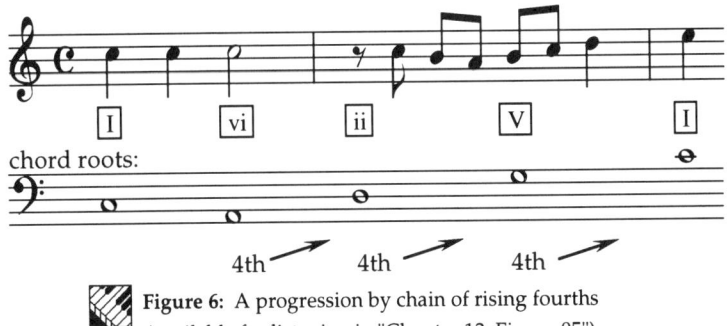

Figure 6: A progression by chain of rising fourths
(available for listening in "Chapter 12, Figure 05")

Progressing backward

Though a sense of resolution comes only with the root movement of a rising fourth, there is still a strong connection when the movement is by a *descending* fourth or *rising* fifth: I often moves to V, of course, and IV to I. Similarly, you may see vi-iii, ii-vi, or even V-ii, as in the Bach chorale of Figure 5.

Root movement by a third

Another extension of the basic chord progression principle comes from the fact that triads whose roots are a third apart sound related, since they always share two notes. Of the two possible ways to move by a third the descending direction seems to be the stronger, perhaps because ascending movement leaves the former root behind:

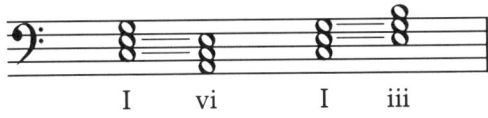

Figure 7: Shared notes in root movement by a third

The stronger kind of movement can effectively be repeated successively at at least once, as in I-vi-IV. It usually isn't so effective to repeat root movement of successive upward thirds (as in vi-I-iii).

Chord substitution and root movement by a second

Because chords whose roots are a third apart sound so similar you can often substitute one for the other. The best example of this is the frequent use of vii° in the place of V. Another case is the "surprise" progression of V to vi, with vi substituting for the expected I. Similarly, the progression IV —V could be seen as based on the very strong ii —V, with IV substituting for ii. Any case of root movement by a second can thus be seen as distantly related to the basic principle of root movement by a fourth.

Until you have enough experience to feel the effectiveness of a particular progression it would probably be safer to limit root movement by a second to one change at a time, as in IV to V or I to ii:

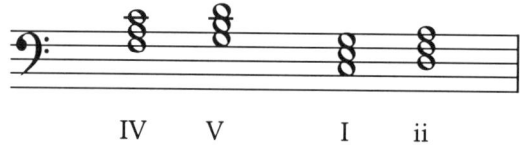

IV   V   I   ii

Figure 8: Root movement by a second

The chord progression game

The above principles are not intended to define all that is possible in harmony. They are a way of describing what tonal composers have usually written in simple pieces. By following these principles your music has a better chance of pleasing you in the same way that you have been pleased by other compositions.

The concepts described above can be summarized in a chart that we will call the "chord board." The "chord board" is for playing a sort of compositional game. To play, you start with any one of the circles numbered "I" for tonic, and then you move to other circles to build a chord progression. Your last chord should be another I, preferably preceded by a V. As in most board games, you can move only in certain ways:

1) You can move along any of the lines that connect chords. Most of the time this means you can move either horizontally, vertically, or diagonally.

2) You can't skip over chords.

3) You can move horizontally rightward any number of times consecutively, but any other direction only twice consecutively at the most.

4) At any time you can jump to a chord of the same name (if you're on a ii spot you can jump to any other ii). This is needed if you reach an edge of the board.

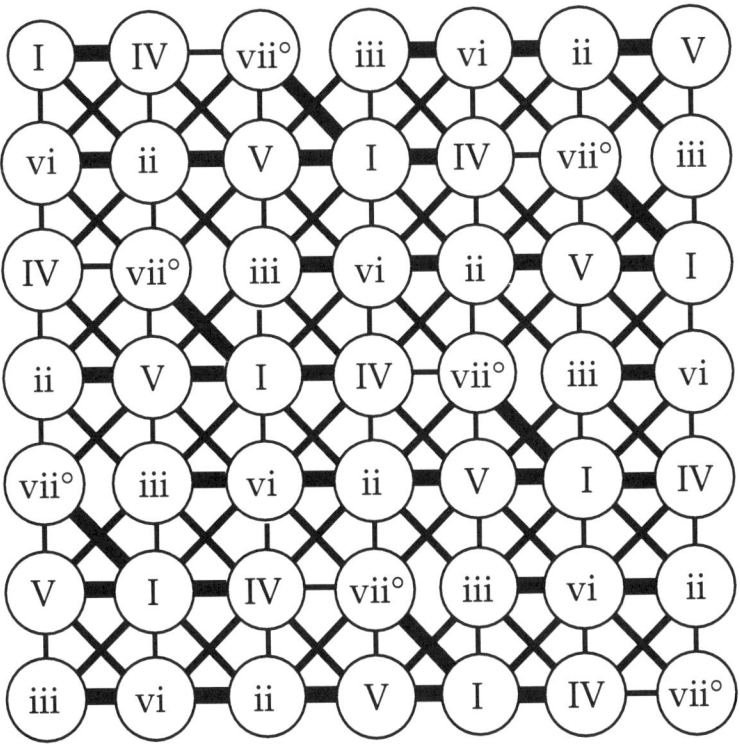

Figure 9: The Chord Board.

The thicker lines are an extra help; they indicate the stronger type of movement. The strong line from vii° to I shows that vii° is used like V to return to the tonic.

The chord board takes no account, of course, of the greater concerns that motivate composers. But it is a fun way to experiment with harmony.

You can use the chord board to make up some progressions for your own amusement, and you might want to try using it to compose a whole song. A similar chord board will work for minor keys:

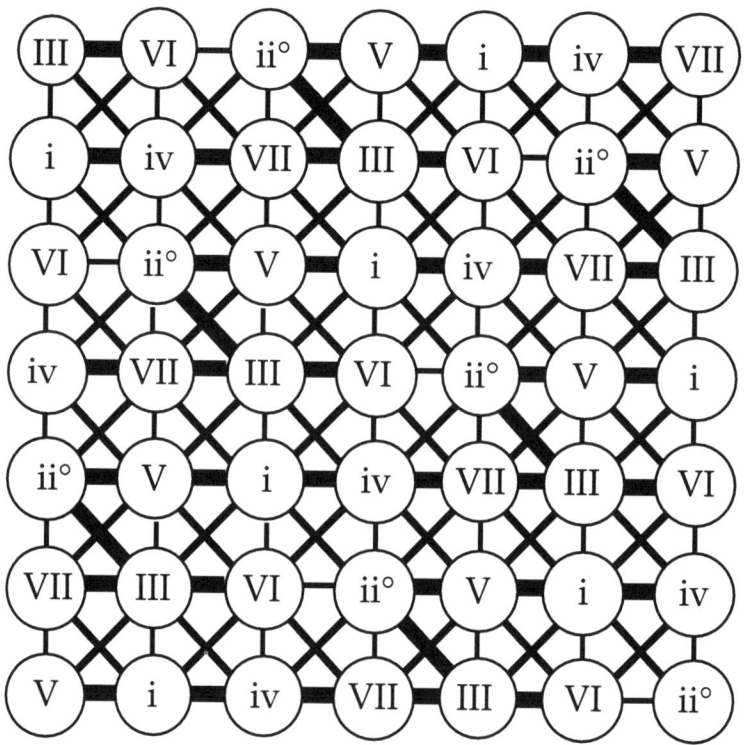

Figure 10: A Chord Board for minor keys

Harmonizing a melody

Even more useful than the ability to construct an isolated chord progression is the ability to figure out what chords would be good accompaniment for an existing melody. This is not so very difficult really, but it will require parts of all the knowledge we have developed so far.

Some melodies signal very clearly which chords underlie them, by outlining those chords melodically:

Figure 11: A melody that outlines chords (from Haydn: *"Surprise" Symphony*)

It's easy to tell such a melody by the fact that it moves mostly by leaps of a third. Two leaps of a third in the same direction will, of course, always spell a triad. Leaps of a fourth or a fifth or a seventh can also be part of an outlined triad:

Figure 12: Another melody that outlines chords

This melody begins with a leap of a fourth from C to F, but the C and F can easily be seen to be part of an F major chord (remember the rule for quick recognition of chords: if you see a perfect fourth the upper note is probably the root of the chord). The last measure has a leap of a seventh and also a leap of a fifth, but both of these fit into a C7 chord, which would be the V7 chord for the key of F.

Nonchordal tones

It is a little harder to see the chords in melodies that include notes that are not meant to be part of the harmony. Such notes are called *nonchordal tones*. However, nonchordal tones usually move by step to a note that *is* part of the chord, and this can help you to recognize them.

Nonchordal tones that come in rhythmically strong positions — for example, on a metric accent or on the first part of a beat subdivision — are called *accented* nonchordal tones. These generally move downward by step to a chord tone. Unaccented nonchordal tones can be found moving either up or down, but again will almost always move by a step to a note that is part of the chord. So if the movement of the melody is upward by step the accented notes are probably part of the chord; if the movement is downward by step the accented notes may or may not be part of the chord, as in this example:

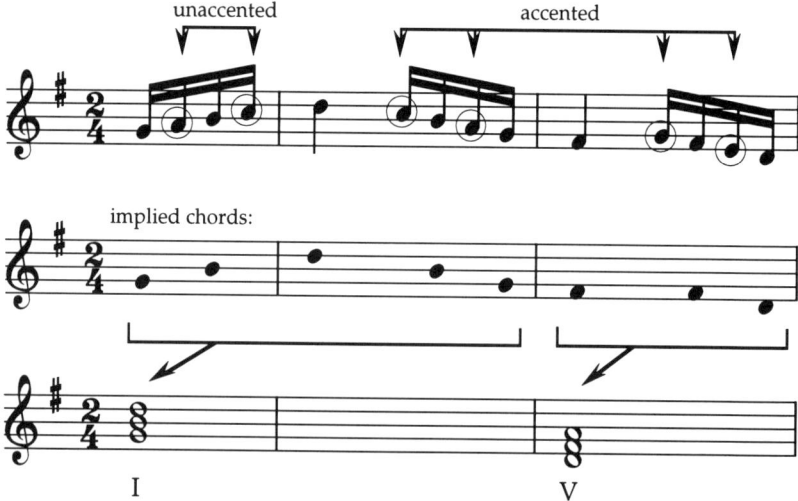

Figure 13: Finding chords in a melody with nonchordal tones (from Clementi: *Rondo*)

It will help in these ambiguous cases to know that most melodies have a slow harmonic rhythm: chords will generally change only twice a bar in 4/4 or even less often. When they do change, the change will almost always occur on the notes with the strongest metric accent: the first beat of the measure, or possibly also the third beat of a 4/4 measure and the second group of three eighthnotes in a 6/8 measure. In the above example the chord changes only once, at the beginning of the third bar. With a typically slow harmonic rhythm a group of sixteenth notes or eighth notes moving stepwise *must* include some nonchordal tones, since you won't be able to change chords fast enough to agree with all of them.

Finally, it is essential to know the typical chord progressions. The F# and D in measure three of the above example could be part of the iii chord or the V, but your first guess should always be the stronger and more common progression, which in this case would be I-V. Also, you can look ahead in a case like this and see that the following chord is again going to be I (not shown above) — and a I-V-I would make much more sense than I-iii-I. In general, V or vii° will tend to be followed by I or possibly vi. Sometimes a return to the I will be interrupted by a IV.

There is almost always more than one good way to harmonize a melody. Guidelines like those above won't help you to choose between the good solutions, but they will help you to avoid the bad ones.

SUPPLEMENTARY TOPICS, CHAPTER X

Secondary dominants

If we want to *really* strengthen those progressions in which the root movement imitates the rising fourth of the dominant—tonic pair we can do various things to make the first chord seem more like a real dominant. A dominant is always a major chord, for one thing, so we can alter minor chords to make them major. The chord ii, for example, which frequently moves to V, can be altered to II, which makes it sound like a "V of V." We call such a fake dominant a *secondary dominant*:

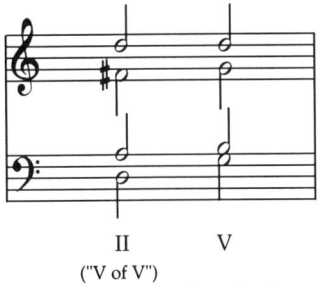

II   V

("V of V")

Figure 14: A secondary dominant

The secondary dominant is still more convincing if we add a minor seventh to it, making it seem exactly like a dominant seventh chord:

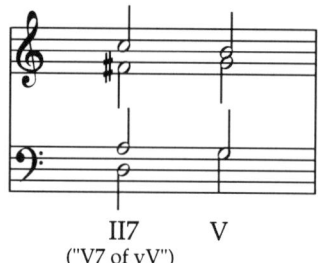

II7   V
("V7 of vV")

Figure 15: A secondary dominant seventh

You can convert any of the triads in a key into secondary dominants, except for the IV:

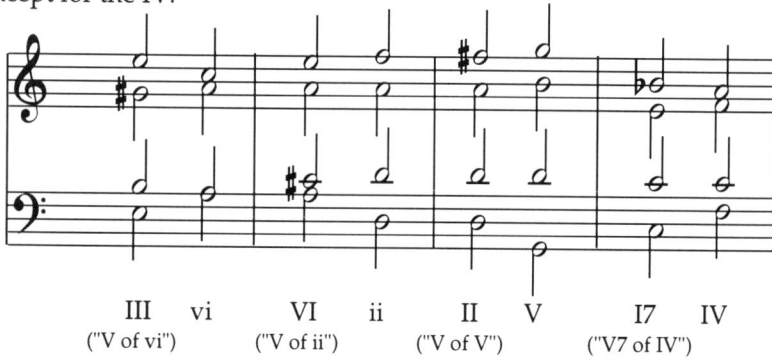

III   vi   VI   ii   II   V   I7   IV
("V of vi")   ("V of ii")   ("V of V")   ("V7 of IV")

Figure 16: A series of secondary dominants in the key of C

Why can't the IV chord function as a secondary dominant? Because the note that is a perfect fourth above IV is a lowered seventh degree (Bb in the key of C), which is not in the scale, and that means that there is no note in the key that could use the IV as its "dominant."

31

Activity

Practica Musica's Chord Ear Training and Chord Progression Ear Training activities will help solidify your understanding of the principles discussed in this chapter.

You should first make sure that you can pass the first two levels of Chord Ear Training. That will bring you to the point where you can easily distinguish the qualities of the basic triads, distinguishing a minor chord from a major one, for example, in different voicings. After that you can go immediately to the first two levels of Chord Progression Ear Training.

While the chord progressions created by Practica Musica are generated at random, they still follow the guidelines presented in this chapter (this may not always be true in the Custom level, or if someone has replaced the standard exercise materials).

In levels 1 and 2 you will learn to hear progressions involving the primary chords I, IV, and V, in major and minor keys. You'll begin, in fact, with only I and V, so that you can gain confidence before moving on. If you have no experience with this you will be surprised how quickly you can learn to identify the primary chords.

For the moment you don't need to go beyond Level 2. Before attempting the higher levels it would be best to round out your knowledge with the material in chapters XI and XIII.

Summary, Chapter X

1. A series of harmonies is called a *chord progression.*

2. The powerful relationship between the dominant and the tonic chords is at the heart of all tonal chord progressions. Other chord pairs can mimic the tonic-dominant relationship and so give impetus to a progression, even when the first of the two is minor. Consequently, the strongest type of chord movement is that in which the roots of the two chords are separated by a fourth or fifth, as they are in the tonic-dominant pair, — especially a rising fourth or descending fifth.

3. The *primary triads* are the tonic, dominant, and subdominant chords. These share a unique and symmetrical relationship wherein the tonic has the same relationship to the subdominant as the dominant has to the tonic. These three are the most important chords in a standard progression.

4. Chords usually change at a relatively slow pace. Most often they change no more than twice in a measure; occasionally they will not change at all for several measures. The speed of the chord changes is called the *harmonic rhythm*.

5. As a general rule, root movement of a rising fourth or descending fifth is strong and effective and may be repeated without limit; other kinds of root movement should not be repeated more than twice successively.

6. To harmonize a melody, follow these principles:

    a. First, look for triads outlined by the melody notes.
    b. Then look for *nonchordal tones* in the melody. These usually involve stepwise movement. Since two notes a step apart cannot be part of the same triad one of them will be a nonchordal tone (for this purpose sevenths, too, are "non chordal tones"). *Accented* nonchordal tones are those in rhythmically strong positions: they usually will move downward by step to a chord tone. *Unaccented* nonchordal tones will also usually move by step to a chordal tone, but they can go up as well as down.
    c. Often two or more chords would harmonize equally well with the notes in a measure; use the chord that would make the best progression *from* the chord of the previous measure and *to* the chord that follows.

Supplementary Topics

7. If a progression involves root movement of a rising fourth the relationship between the two chords can be made even stronger by making the first one into a *secondary dominant*. This is done by altering the chord (if it needs it) to make it major and perhaps also by adding a minor seventh to make a "dominant seventh" chord. The result mimics the relationship between the dominant and tonic. If a chord is altered in this way it is referred to as "V (or V7) of x," where x is the second chord. The ii chord, for example, can be made into "V of V."

XI. BUILDING MELODIES

No one has ever been able to adequately describe what makes a successful melody. Yet we can list some superficial characteristics that are shared by good melodies, and these may at least help you to make tunes that are not awkward. We'll examine several melodies and discuss these aspects of each one:

1) The way that it moves.
2) The way its ideas are organized into *phrases*.
3) The way it develops musical ideas.

Melodic movement

Great and memorable melodies are often ones that are easy to sing, even if they are meant to be played by an instrument. Perhaps we find a tune more enjoyable if we can imagine singing it —or perhaps the qualities that make something easy to sing are also valuable aesthetically. This famous melody from Brahms' First Symphony, for example, could easily be a song with words although it was written to be played by an orchestra:

Figure 1: From Johannes Brahms' *Symphony No. 1 (see Figure 10 for listening)*

We could begin by thinking about the characteristics that make a melody easy to sing. The excerpt from Brahms will serve as a good example.

First, Brahms' melody has a limited *range*. In other words, it never gets very far away in pitch from where it started. The excerpt above is confined to the notes within a seventh. Most famous melodies stay within an octave, or at most an octave plus a third or fourth.

Secondly, the movement is mostly by step, with some small *leaps* (a leap is defined as any interval larger than a second). No leap in this melody is larger than a fifth, and even that leap marks a dividing point in the tune (measure 4). If you would like your melody to have a similar flowing quality be sure to use mostly *stepwise movement*, with occasional small leaps.

Thirdly, leaps larger than a fourth tend to be *compensated* by an immediate move in the other direction, and in most great melodies leaps larger than a fifth or at most a sixth are rare unless they are octaves. Even when the leap is small, singable melodies rarely leap twice in a row in the same direction, *unless the notes involved are all part of the same triad.*

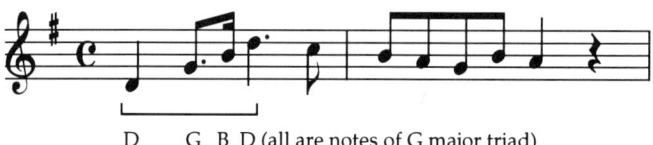

D   G B D (all are notes of G major triad)

Figure 2: Consecutive leaps outlining a triad

Fourthly, all intervals in the Brahms melody are major or minor or perfect — there are no augmented or diminished intervals. Use of an augmented or diminished interval in a melody is not unknown, but it is unusual, and it is more difficult for a singer.

Finally, the rhythm of a great tune tends to be fairly simple. A melody with many fast notes is difficult to sing, as are rhythms with many stops and starts. A general rule for melodic rhythm is this — could you imagine singing words to it? If not, maybe it won't work very well even without words.

You might compare the examples below. The first is the beginning of *My Country, 'Tis of Thee*. The second example has the same meter and the same number of notes, but it moves in ways that violate the above principles. It would be very difficult to sing and probably would not appeal to many listeners. Roughly speaking, the second one "jumps around too much."

Figure 3: A popular tune and one that probably won't be popular
(Available for listening)

32

Activity

Select Melody Writing/Listening from your Practica Musica Activities menu, and then open the musical examples for figures 03a and 03b, as pictured above. Listen to each one, and try to sing with each. What do you think? Surely you can improve upon the second example.

Try changing the pitches of the second example to make it easier to sing. Essentially you'll be writing your own tune using the rhythms of *My Country 'tis of thee.* Select the pitch slider tool,🎵, place it on a note you want to change, and then drag it up or down with the mouse button depressed. This will change the note's pitch without altering its rhythmic value.

Try to make a melody that stays within an octave, that moves mostly by steps, that avoids leaps larger than a sixth, that compensates any leaps of a fifth or sixth, and that avoids movement by augmented or diminished leaps such as the one from F to B. Don't use any accidentals for now: stick to the notes of the scale. Here's an example of the sort of tune you might write:

(cont'd next page)

If you like the sound of your tune you should try to carry it on further to make a complete song. To do that, though, you will need to know how melodic ideas are developed.

Melodic ideas and their development

A good melody is more than just something that is singable. If a great melody could be written by merely following the above rules then even Practica Musica could write one — but the tunes invented by Practica Musica seem to wander around in a pleasant way without really saying anything meaningful (sometimes they will sound meaningful, but if so it's just good luck: a machine cannot have anything to say, after all). Perhaps we should compare the Brahms melody with one invented by the computer, to see if we can discover why the first sounds meaningful and the other is only amusing.

Below is a tune invented by Practica Musica. It follows the above rules for melodic movement, but it is not likely to give competition to Brahms. Is there anything specific you could name that the Brahms melody has and this one lacks?

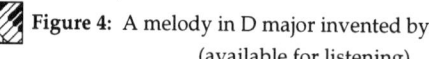 **Figure 4:** A melody in D major invented by Practica Musica
(available for listening)

One big difference is that the machine-made melody has no *repetition,* whereas the last four measures of the Brahms are almost the same as the first four:

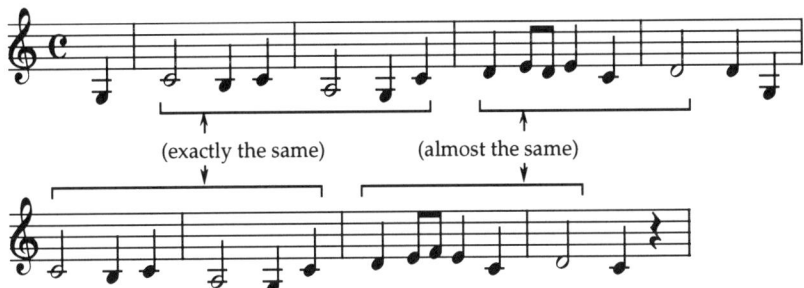

Figure 5: Repetition in the Brahms melody

My Country, 'tis of Thee also includes two measures that closely resemble others:

Figure 6: Varied repetition in *My Country, 'tis of Thee*

Music depends a great deal on repetition. Listening to a piece of music is a little like hearing a story told in a new language whose words are taught to you as you go along. The teaching is done through repetition of melody fragments, of melodies, of chord progressions, of whole sections.

Often the repetition is not exact: it may involve some kind of variation or development of the original idea. The third measure of the Brahms tune is slightly varied when it returns, and the third and fourth measures of *My Country, 'tis of Thee* represent a more extensive variation or development of the idea that formed the first two measures. In both tunes this development of a previous idea helps to give the listener the impression that the melody is a unified whole rather than just a string of unrelated notes. The melody invented by Practica Musica, on the other hand, presented several "ideas" but didn't do anything with them — it just wandered on to other ideas. That shows a certain lack of appreciation for its own work, which is part of the reason why the computer is no threat to the livelihood of human composers. Later in this chapter we'll discuss various of the techniques a human composer uses to extend and develop melodic ideas.

The phrase

Another characteristic of the Brahms tune is that it clearly divides into *phrases*. The musical phrase is like a phrase in language, but it is even more like a line of poetry. It is separated from the next phrase by a form of musical punctuation that has an effect much like the end of a poetic line, often producing a slight pause or the taking of a breath.

Figure 7: Phrases in the Brahms melody

The beginning of the second phrase in the Brahms is easy to see because the second phrase is basically a repetition of the first one. If you could hear and understand the harmonies implied by the tune (you'll eventually be able to do this) you would also notice a harmonic change that marks the end of this first phrase. The tune begins on the tonic chord, passes through the subdominant, and at the end of the phrase comes to rest on the dominant. The "incomplete" feeling associated with the dominant tells the listener that more is to come. The second phrase, on the other hand, ends on a solid tonic chord, marking the end of a neat musical "statement." Such endings of phrases are sometimes called "open" and "closed" endings. The closed ending must finish on a note of the tonic chord while the open ending should finish on a different note, often one of those that make up the dominant chord.

The first two phrases of "Twinkle, twinkle little star" form a pair, the first of which has an open ending and the second a closed ending:

Figure 8: First two phrases in "Twinkle, twinkle"

The two-measure phrases that begin *My Country, 'Tis of Thee* are another open-closed pair (see Figure 6).

The period

Each of the phrase pairs above could be called a *period*, which is roughly analogous to a complete sentence in spoken language. A period is two or more phrases that make a natural group, the last one having a closed ending.

Cadences

The effect of an "open" ending and a "closed" one is produced by the *cadence* at the end of each phrase. A cadence is a real or implied chord change that provides a kind of harmonic punctuation at a phrase ending, just as a comma or a semicolon can end a phrase in verbal language. An open ending is produced by a cadence to the V, which is known as an *incomplete cadence* or a *half-cadence*. The more final-sounding V—I is called the *authentic cadence*, which makes a closed ending. Another final cadence is the IV—I, called the *plagal cadence* (*plagal* derives from the Greek word for "oblique" or "slanting," perhaps because a plagal cadence seems to be less solid than the authentic cadence).

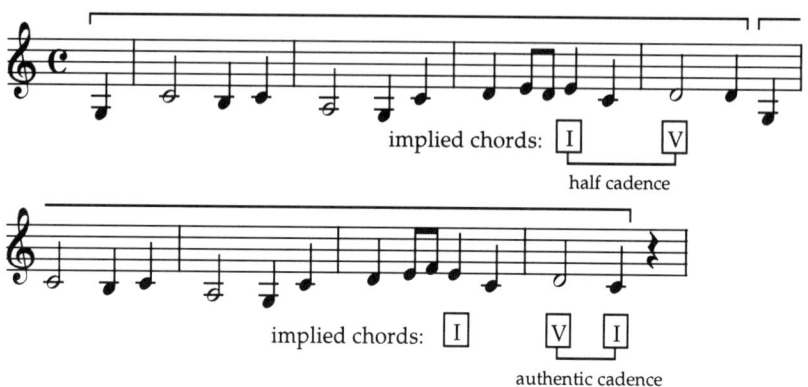

Figure 9: A half cadence and an authentic cadence

Harmonic implications of melody

This talk of cadences has entered us on an important aspect of melody: its implied harmony. A successful melody in the tonal style will tend to suggest harmonies that make a strong chord progression. The Brahms tune, for example, seems to demand the harmony given it by its composer, a very clear and solid progression using I, IV, and V:

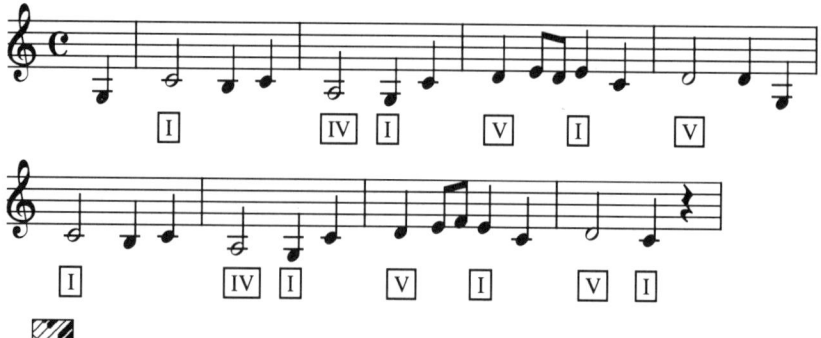

Figure 10: Complete chords for Brahms' melody (available for listening)

My Country, 'tis of Thee also carries a chord progression that is firm and logical. It could be harmonized with just I, IV, and V, but often secondary chords and even the "V7 of vi" are added, making a strong chain-of-fourths progression:

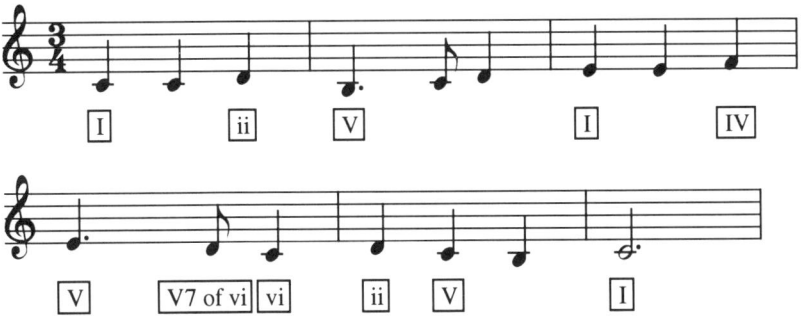

 Figure 11: Chords for *My Country, 'tis of Thee* (available for listening)

What sort of chord progression could be made to go with the "awkward" tune we wrote earlier? That tune wouldn't be very easy to harmonize: the chords would need to change often and they wouldn't make a very strong series. It would be hard to come up with a tonal harmonization much better than this:

Figure 12: This one doesn't allow a good chord progression (available for listening)

It's interesting that two of our three principles for melody writing are closely related: the rules of movement that make a melody easy to sing have the effect of making it easier to harmonize, too. The preference for stepwise motion and for leaps that outline triads naturally allows dissonance resolution and produces a slow harmonic rhythm.

SUPPLEMENTARY TOPICS, CHAPTER XI

Techniques of melodic development

Now you have some superficial guides that can help make a melody easy to sing and comprehensible. It would help to know more about how your melodic ideas can be extended and developed.

There are some very specific ways that a melodic idea can be varied while still keeping a recognizable connection with its former shape. Knowledge of these techniques is an important part of the composer's skill, though some of them are often used unconsciously and can even be found in many folk melodies.

Below is a traditional children's song that illustrates some of the techniques used to develop melodic ideas.

Figure 13: "Lightly Row " (available for listening)

The sequence

Doesn't the first measure resemble measure two? Plainly, measure two is the same three-note melody played a step lower. In the same way, the notes of measures 11-12 make the same pattern as those in measures 9-10, but a step higher. This is a type of variation called the *sequence*, in which the pattern of a melody is simply repeated at a different pitch level. Some of the steps and leaps may be slightly different, but the shape of the melody remains the same. Sequences can be carried on as far as you like, though they tend to sound silly if they continue too long. For example, three times is pushing the limit for this idea:

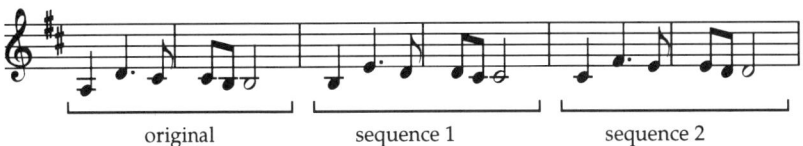

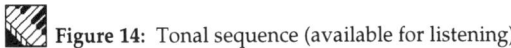

 Figure 14: Tonal sequence (available for listening)

Notice the slight changes in the intervals of this tune. For example, the step following the dotted quarter is a minor second originally, but a major second in both of the sequences. That is because this most common type of sequence, the *tonal sequence*, uses no accidentals. If the original goes up a second then the sequence goes up a second, but without accidentals it may turn out that the second is minor instead of major, or vice-versa.

The other kind of sequence is the *real* sequence, which preserves exactly the shape of the original melody by adding accidentals. This means that the sequence will soon move into other scales, which is often undesirable:

Figure 15: Real sequence (available for listening)

33 **Activity**

Select Melody Writing from your Practica Musica Activities menu, and then begin a New Melody. Use the boxes above the screen keyboard to choose the key of C major and the common-time meter "C" (4/4) as below.

Enter the following melodic idea. Choose the notes or other symbols you want by clicking on them and then click in the staff where you want them to appear. (Choosing the arrow key will allow you to select notes and symbols for deletion, if necessary. The Autobeam button will convert your flagged eighthnotes to beamed eighthnotes.)

Can you write tonal sequences of this? Below is what an ascending sequence at the second would look like. Try writing another sequence one second higher than that and then play it. Can you identify which steps have changed from major to minor or from minor to major? Listen again carefully after you identify them, and try to *hear* the difference.

Then delete your work (or save it and make a new melody) and try some descending sequences. The idea below would work well if sequenced down by thirds. Notice that it uses a different meter:

Finally, invent an idea of your own and make several sequences ascending or descending.

The motive

The first sequence in *Lightly Row* is based on a three-note pattern that appears frequently in the song — in fact, 9 of the 16 measures consist of repetitions or variations of this same small idea, which can be called a *motive*:

the motive   transposed down   preserving rhythm
                                              and repeated notes

Figure 16: Motive from "Lightly Row"

A motive is a short, distinctive fragment of melody, or even just a rhythm, that appears repeatedly in recognizable form. The sequence in measure two of "Lightly Row" is an example of a motive being varied by *transposition*, whereas measure four is a variation that preserves only the rhythm and the repeated notes of the motive. In measures ten and twelve you can find a still more distant variation that discards even the repeated notes and keeps the rhythm only.

One of the most famous motives of all time is the one Beethoven used to begin his Fifth Symphony:

Figure 17: Motive from Beethoven's Fifth Symphony

The motive in this case is four notes: three that repeat and one that descends a third. This pattern, sometimes reduced to just its rhythm, appears in many different forms throughout the work:

Figure 18: Some variants of Beethoven's motive

Regular transformations

There are four regular (i.e., mechanical) operations that can change a motive or an entire melody into something that has a family resemblance to the original: they are *transposition, inversion, retrograde,* and *retrograde inversion.* For all of these transformations we'll consider only the tonal forms, which, like the tonal sequence, aren't exact.

Transposition we've already seen in the sequence: the melodic idea is played at a different pitch level. Some minor intervals might become major and major ones minor, but the shape of the melody is retained.

To make an *inversion* of a melody you just go up where the original went down. The below motive rises two seconds and then drops a third and a fourth, so its inversion descends two seconds and then rises a third and a fourth:

original   inversion

Figure 19: Melodic inversion

A *retrograde* variation is the reverse of the original. Sometimes only the pitches are reversed; sometimes the rhythm is reversed as well. You may recognize this retrograde of part of a well-known tune:

Figure 20: Retrograde (rhythm and pitch)

Finally, you can make a variation that is both backwards and inverted: a *retrograde inversion*:

Figure 21: Retrograde inversion of the same melody

Two types of rhythmic variation

There are also regular changes that can be made in rhythmic patterns. Like the regular transformations of pitch patterns, these rhythmic transformations produce a variant whose connection with the original can be easily recognized.

The rhythm could be made in larger values (*rhythmic augmentation*), as with this version of the Beethoven motive:

Figure 22: Rhythmic augmentation

Ot it could be made in shorter values (*rhythmic diminution*):

Figure 23: Rhythmic diminution

Elaboration

The regular transformations are seldom used in the mechanical fashion described above, except for brief passages. More often, transformed material is freely varied at the same time. One type of free development is *elaboration*, in which extra notes are added to the melody. Sometimes the rhythms and pitches will be changed freely as well, to the point where you may scarcely recognize the original idea. You may have more trouble hearing the Beethoven motive in the below (he didn't write this):

Figure 24: An elaboration of the Beethoven motive

An example

Here is an illustration of how the above techniques can produce a great deal of music from a single motive:

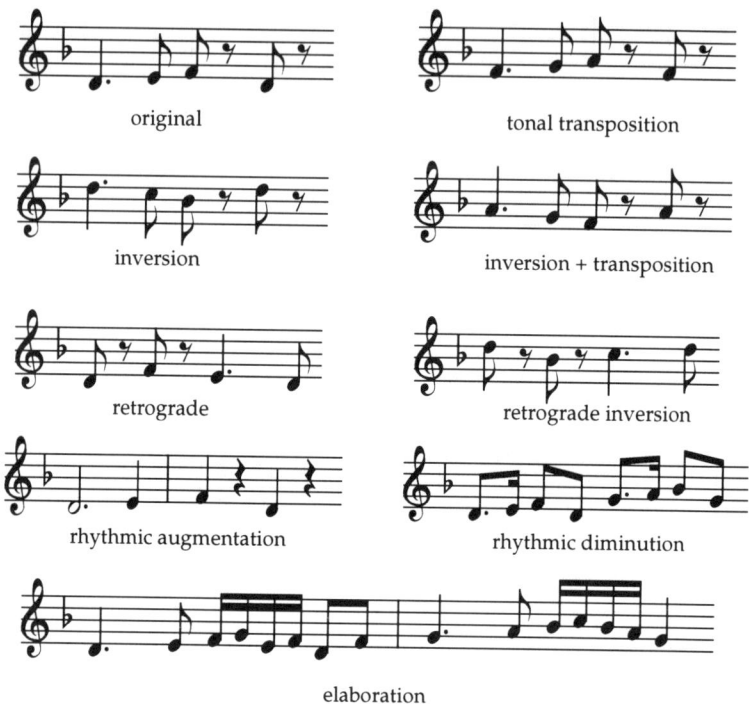

Figure 25: Developing a single idea (available for listening)

So far we've looked at the type of movement usually found in a good melody, the way its ideas are expressed in phrases, and various of the ways that a single small idea can be extended and developed. This first part of the task might be compared to the design of parts for a sculpture or a building. Next comes the task of building these parts into a larger structure.

Summary, Chapter XI.

1. Memorable melodies are often ones that are easily singable, even if they are not intended to be sung.

2. Some qualities that make a tune singable are 1) range limited to an octave 2) mostly stepwise motion, 3) leaps greater than a 4th compensated by immediate movement in the opposite direction, 4) few augmented or diminished leaps, 5) simple rhythm.

3. A melodic *phrase* is generally two to four measures in length; it corresponds to a phrase of language or a line of poetry and is sometimes set off in performance by a taking of breath or a slight pause.

4. A *cadence* is the chord change that marks the end of a phrase. A V-I cadence is called an *incomplete* or *half* cadence; it produces an "open" effect. The V-I cadence is called the *authentic* cadence and the IV-I the *plagal* cadence; both of these produce a "closed" ending to the phrase, since they end on the tonic. Phrases often come in pairs, one of which may end with an open ending and the other with a closed ending. The two together can be called a *period*.

5. A successful tonal melody will usually imply a strong chord progression with a slow harmonic rhythm.

6. Successful melodies often are built from only a few basic ideas that are repeated and developed.

Supplementary topics

7. The *sequence* is a technique of developing a brief melodic idea by transposing it up or down one or more times in succession. Usually it is transposed by a second or a third.

8. The *tonal sequence* allows the quality of melodic intervals to change according to the key (i.e., it does not use accidentals to maintain the quality of each interval). The *real sequence* represents an exact transposition of the original pattern and will usually require the use of accidentals.

9. A *motive* is a small melodic or rhythmic idea that is varied and developed and extended in a composition.

10. The *regular transformations* are ways of mechanically changing a tune or a rhythm so that it is different and yet clearly related to the original. *Transposition* repeats a pitch pattern at a higher or lower starting point; *inversion* changes the direction of each interval in the melody; *retrograde* reverses the tune, and *retrograde inversion* both inverts it and reverses it. Regular transformations of rhythm include *augmentation*, in which each note is increased in value by the same proportion, and *diminution*, in which the notes are all diminished by the same proportion.

11. *Elaboration* is a free development of a melodic idea, adding additional notes and perhaps altering the pattern in other ways.

XII. ELEMENTS OF FORM

Binary and ternary song forms

We are now prepared to look again at the song "Lightly Row," this time to consider the pattern made by its phrases. A common way to study phrase patterns is to label each phrase with a letter, similar phrases being given the same letter:

Figure 1. Rounded binary form: *Lightly Row*
(available for listening under Chapter 11, Figure 13)

The phrases show the pattern AA'BA'. The first two phrases are a matched pair in which the first has an open ending and the second a closed ending (sometimes called an *antecedent—consequent* phrase pair). In the letter diagram the accent mark on the second "A" indicates that the two phrases have different cadences. Then follows a contrasting phrase marked B, which has an open ending, and finally a closed version of the A phrase returns to end the verse.

Many other songs and dances share this form, which is known as *rounded binary*. It's called binary (two-part) because it divides in halves, and it's "rounded" in that a portion of the first half returns at the end. The most important thing about it is the return of the beginning material at the end, which is an idea found in much larger works. The return makes this almost a *ternary* (three-part) form, a clearer example of which is "Twinkle, twinkle, little star:"

Figure 2: Ternary form: *Twinkle, twinkle, little star* (available for listening)

If the tune from the first phrase didn't return the form would be simple binary, as in "Greensleeves:"

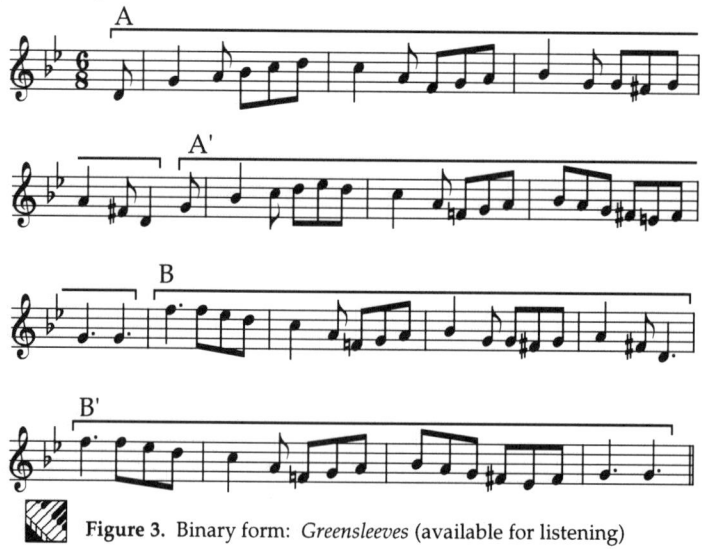

Figure 3. Binary form: *Greensleeves* (available for listening)

All of the above forms share one characteristic: they are built from two contrasting elements, A and B. Sometimes A and B are repeated, sometimes not; sometimes A returns again after B and sometimes it does not.

Other songs, however, are made from nothing more than a single phrase pair, such as this one:

Figure 4. A song consisting of a single period (available for listening)

Almost any simple traditional or popular song will have one of the above forms of organization, or something closely resembling one of them. However, there are also other types of musical organization based on completely different principles, and we will look at several of those next.

Some other forms of organization: the *chaconne*

The *chaconne*, in the time of Bach, was an instrumental piece in a slow triple meter built on a repeated chord progression. The chaconne technique survives today in much popular instrumental and vocal music in which a simple progression is repeated while the melody changes and develops. Though it is not in triple meter, "Heart and Soul" might be considered a sort of modern chaconne:

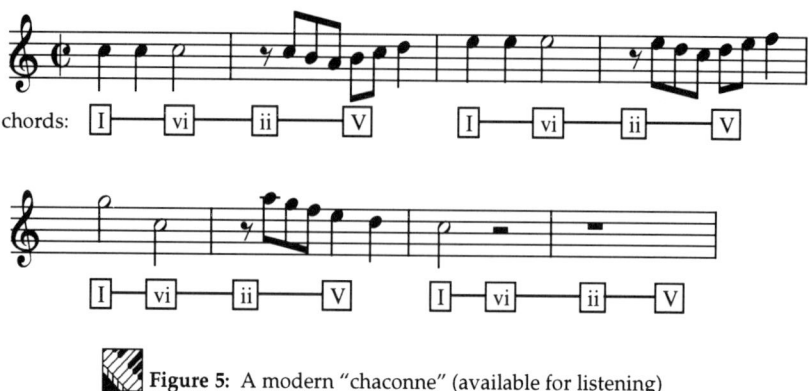

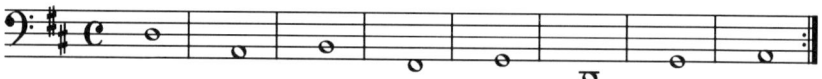

Figure 5: A modern "chaconne" (available for listening)

Ostinato and the *passacaglia*

Strictly speaking, a chaconne repeats only the chord progression itself, while the bass melody may vary. Other pieces may repeat the bass melody exactly, forming an *ostinato bass*. The word *passacaglia* , though sometimes used interchangeably with "chaconne," can specifically apply to works built on an ostinato. In Pachelbel's well-known Canon in D, which could be described as a combination canon and passacaglia, the bass player is given the task of repeating this ostinato pattern 57 times!

Figure 6: An ostinato bass

The other voices of the Pachelbel Canon are complicated; this simple repeating pattern in the bass helps to make the composition easier to understand.

Canon and round

One of the most enjoyable group activities for students of music is the singing of canons and rounds. A canon is a tune that is carefully designed to harmonize with itself when two or more performers sing it starting at different times. Probably the best-known of these is "Row, row, row your boat," which is a special type of canon known as a *round*

— a canon whose ending harmonizes with its beginning and which therefore can repeat without stopping. Here's another round that works very well and which you may not know:

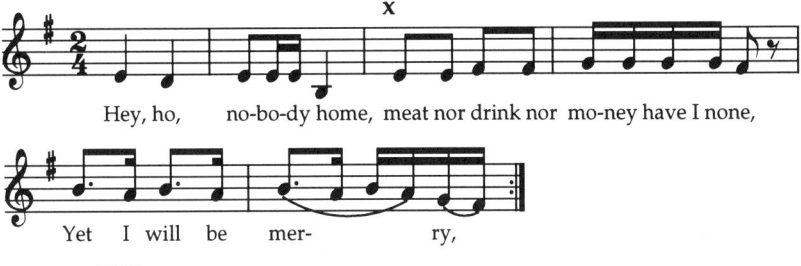

Figure 7. An old English round (available for listening)

This round can be sung in three parts. The second singer begins when the first one reaches the "x," and the third singer begins when the second singer reaches the "x." Each singer on reaching the end goes immediately to the beginning again without missing a beat. You can see the effect of this more clearly if we write out the first bars as they would be heard. This would be called writing the music *in score*, so that all the sounding parts can be seen together:

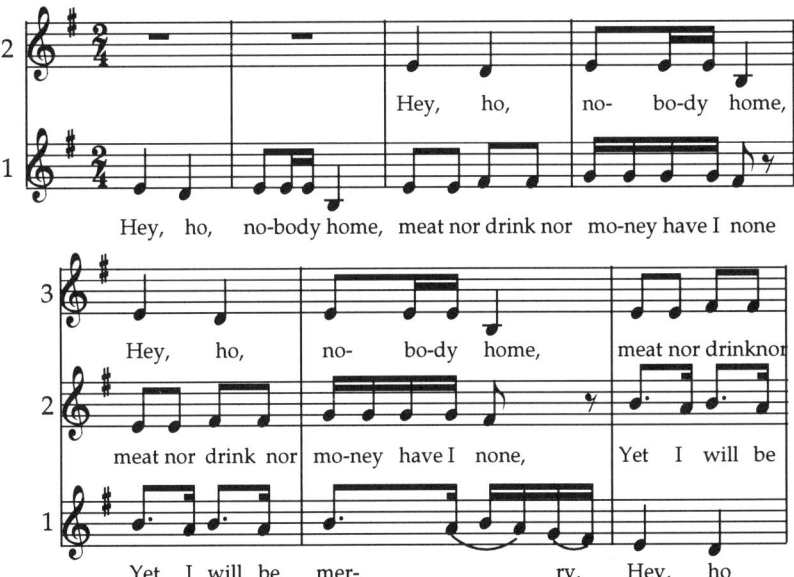

Figure 8. Part of "Hey, ho" in score (singers numbered 1, 2, 3)

34

Activity

Select Melody Writing/Listening from the Practica Musica activities menu, and then open the example for Chapter 12, Figure 07.

Now we can make use of a special Practica Musica feature that will enable you to sing this round in two parts together with the computer. Hold down the Cloverleaf key (just to the right of the Option key on your Macintosh keyboard) and press "R." Now when you ask Practica Musica to play the melody it will repeat endlessly until you press the spacebar.

Singing a round takes some practice at first, because you may be confused by the fact that the other singer is "in a different place" in the melody. Listen carefully to the melody until you feel that you know it well. Then start singing it yourself from the beginning when Practica Musica reaches the first note of measure three (the word, "meat," if the computer could sing words). Once you can do this with the machine try it with a human!

SUPPLEMENTARY TOPICS, CHAPTER XII

Large forms: the symphony

In the above examples of small forms the letters have represented just single phrases. If we instead use letters to represent longer passages of music we can see how these simple formal ideas are also involved in the making of large pieces. As an example we'll discuss the classical *symphony*, a large composition for orchestra. The symphony is typically divided into four sections or *movements*, each of which traditionally has a particular form.

Sonata form

The phrase structure of "Lightly row" is a very distant relative of the plan for the first movement of most classical symphonies, which, although much more complicated, is still basically a rounded binary form in which the beginning material returns at the end.

This form, called *sonata form*, is probably more important than any other in classical music. It is always used for the first movement of a sonata, and almost all the major classical works are sonatas: symphonies are sonatas for orchestra, string quartets are sonatas for quartet, concertos are sonatas for a solo instrument and orchestra.

The divisions within a sonata are based on more than just similar melodies, however. The sonata is organized around its *key*, which changes in the course of each section. The first section, called the *exposition*, presents melodies in the tonic key and then *modulates* (changes key), usually to the key of the dominant. So, for example, a sonata in C major would be in G major at the end of the exposition. The next section, called the *development*, will often use some of the techniques described in Chapter XI to modify and vary the melodic material presented in the exposition, and it may also modulate to a number of other keys. The end of the development will be marked by a return of the melodies heard at the beginning, in their original key. But this *recapitulation* will be rewritten so that it doesn't modulate to the dominant — this time it will end on the tonic.

Exposition	Development	Recapitulation
Modulate to dominant	Dominant and other keys	Back to tonic
Themes: x, y	develop x, y	return of x,y

Figure 9. Typical sonata form

Theme and variations

The second movement of a symphony is usually slow and cast in an expanded version of the binary or ternary form found in songs. Sometimes, however, a composer may choose to write a *Theme and Variations*. The theme, usually a folk song or other well-known melody, will be played through once in its plain form and will then be played a number of additional times with various alterations. The goal of the composer is to change the music in interesting ways while still allowing the listener to recognize the theme. Though not from a symphony, the following is a particularly clear example of variation. You should be able to recognize the tune we know as "Twinkle, Twinkle, little star" in this excerpt:

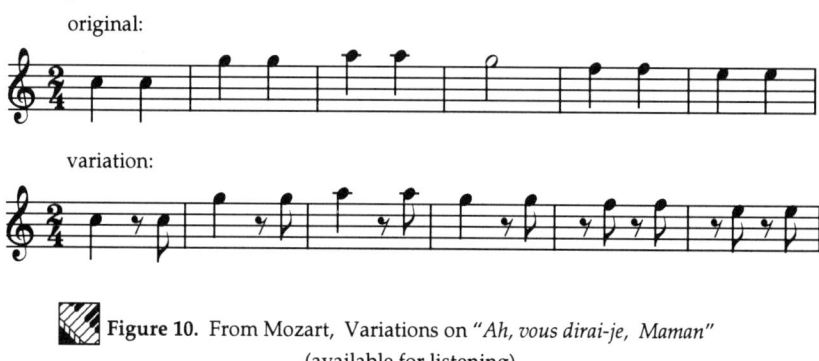

Figure 10. From Mozart, Variations on *"Ah, vous dirai-je, Maman"* (available for listening)

Most variations will include one in which the key is changed from major to minor or vice-versa, and most will include variations that elaborate the melody with many quick added notes. The meter may be changed in some variations, for example, converting "Twinkle" to 6/8. The possibilities are limited only by the imagination of the composer.

Minuet and trio

The third movement of a symphony is almost always a pair of dances in triple meter, called a *Minuet and Trio*. The Minuet and Trio displays both binary and ternary form, since each dance is in rounded binary form and the movement as a whole is ternary — the trio serves as the middle section and the minuet is repeated afterward. A typical Minuet and Trio could be represented as follows:

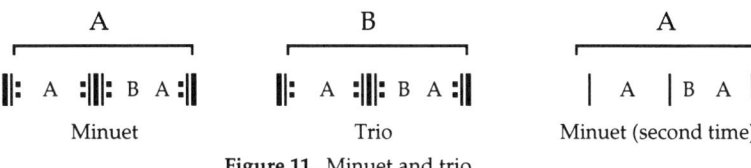

Figure 11. Minuet and trio

When the minuet is played for the last time its repeats are left out. There is more to this form than just the mechanical structure: usually the Minuet has the more vigorous dance-like rhythms, while the Trio has a contrasting lyrical (song-like) character.

The Rondo

Finally, the last movement of the symphony may appear as a *rondo*, which has a shape resembling ABACADA. That pattern can be compared to a repeated ternary form, except that again each letter refers to a much larger musical passage and the "B" is constantly being replaced by new material: C, D, etc. The distinguishing feature of the rondo is the repeated return of the A material, which is usually an easily recognizable passage. Between the first A and the final one the rondo will modulate to other keys, as did the sonata.

These are just the barest outlines of the larger forms, but should be enough to help you recognize them. Remember, though, that these designs are just the most typical patterns; there is a great deal of variation in these forms and there are other patterns that have grown out of them. The ingenuity employed by composers in shaping large works is a subject that can be studied in great depth.

Summary, Chapter XII

1. The binary and ternary song forms are built from contrasting phrases or phrase groups, which in diagrams are represented as A and B. The *binary* song form can be represented as AA'BB', where the accents mark a closed phrase ending. The *rounded binary* song substitutes a return of the A material in place of the second B, as in AA'BA'. The *ternary* song has three parts: ABA. These forms can be expanded: in a simple folk song each letter may refer to only a single phrase; in a larger composed song the letter may stand for a phrase group or a still larger section of music.

2. Other ways of organizing music include schemes of repeating chord progressions or repeating melodies. A piece built on a repeating chord progression can be called a *chaconne*. A *passacaglia* is based on a repeated melody that is usually in the bass but can appear in other voices. Such a repeated accompaniment melody is itself called an *ostinato*.

3. The word *canon* generally refers to a tune that is written so that it can provide its own accompaniment. One player begins the tune and after the first player has reached a certain point another one joins in, playing from the start. A *round* is a special kind of canon whose ending harmonizes its beginning, so that it can be repeated endlessly.

Supplementary topics

4. If the letters used to analyze phrase structures are applied to larger passages, we can see that large pieces of music often have forms that are distant relatives of the basic song forms. Several important large forms are included in the classical *symphony*, a work for orchestra that is usually divided into four *movements* or sections.

5. The first movement of a classical symphony is almost always in *sonata form*, which resembles a greatly expanded rounded binary form. The typical sonata form is based on harmonic organization: the first half, the *exposition*, modulates to the dominant; the next half begins with a *development* section that starts in the dominant and may pass through other keys, and that is followed by the *recapitulation*, again in the tonic key and featuring material from the first section. The recapitulation corresponds to the return of the A in rounded binary form.

6. The second movement of a symphony is usually a slow movement built on an expanded song form. In some cases it may be a *Theme and Variations*, in which you hear first a simple, usually well-known, melody and then many variations of it. The goal in such a movement is to vary the tune in interesting ways while still allowing it to be recognized.

7. The third movement is traditionally a Minuet and Trio, two dances based on rounded binary form. The minuet is usually the most vigorous and dance-like, with the trio having a contrasting lyrical character. After the Trio the minuet is played again (without repeats, this time), so that the movement as a whole also has an ABA form.

8. The last movement of a symphony is frequently a *Rondo,* which has a form resembling ABACADA. The essential characterisitic is the repeated returns of the A material.

XIII. ADDING TO THE TRIAD

More About Seventh chords

The major and minor triads are consonant and stable; they seem to be at rest. The diminished and augmented triads are dissonant and therefore restless; when you hear one of them you might assume that more is yet to come.

That desirable sense of instability is produced whenever dissonant notes are included in harmony. As mentioned in Chapter IX, one dissonance that is particularly common is the interval of a seventh formed with a chord's root. This seventh can be seen as an extension of the basic structure of the triad — it's like another third placed on top. The four notes together make a *seventh chord*:

Figure 1: Some seventh chords

The seventh that appears most often in tonal harmony is a minor seventh added to the dominant triad. This sonority can be seen in general terms as a major triad with a minor third on top, and so it is sometimes called the *major minor seventh chord*. We call it the *dominant seventh chord* to show its origins, since it is found naturally only on the dominant degree in a major scale.

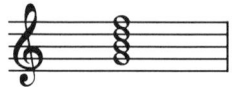

Figure 2: The dominant seventh chord for the key of C

Observe that by adding a seventh to the dominant triad we have actually introduced two dissonances: a seventh between the outer notes and a diminished fifth between the seventh and the third. These can be easily seen if we display all of the intervals contained within the dominant seventh:

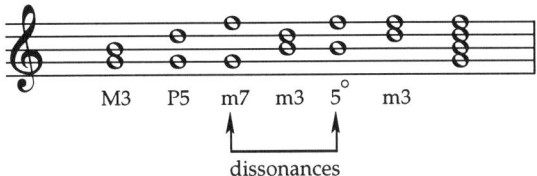

Figure 3: Dissonances in the dominant seventh chord

If we voice the chord differently these dissonances may change names: the minor seventh can invert to a second, for example. But the effect of instability will be the same.

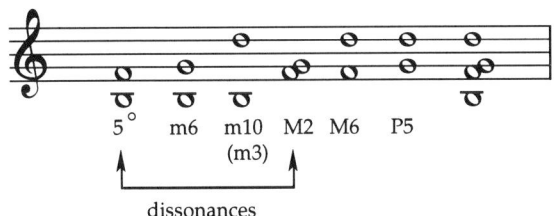

Figure 4: A rearranged (inverted) dominant seventh chord

Resolving dissonances

As mentioned earlier, a dissonant interval is traditionally *resolved to* a consonant one. In modern music dissonant chords are often left unresolved, but in the works of composers such as Mozart or Beethoven a dissonant chord introduces a consonant one. There are a few conventions of dissonance resolution that are interesting with regard to the use of seventh chords: 1) the upper note of a seventh usually moves downward by a step; 2) a second often expands to form a third, usually by moving its lower note downward; 3) a diminished interval will often contract to the nearest consonance, and 4) an augmented interval will often expand to the nearest consonance. The following are some typical resolutions:

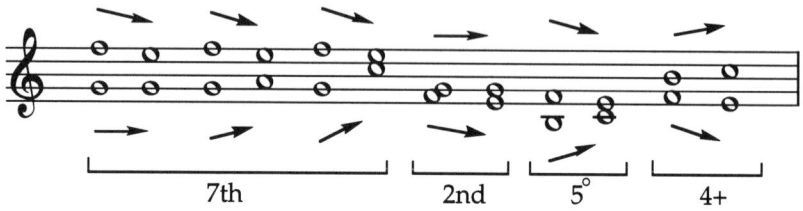

| 7th | 2nd | 5° | 4+ |

Figure 5: Typical resolutions of dissonant intervals

Suppose we apply these conventional resolutions to the dissonances within the dominant seventh chord for C major. To demonstrate we'll voice the chords with four parts, with the root doubled:

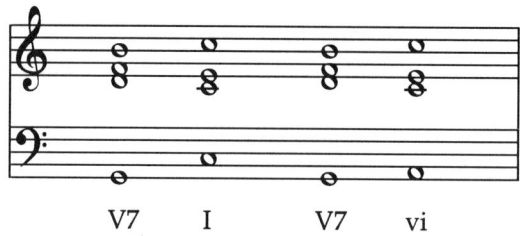

V7   I   V7   vi

Figure 6: Two resolutions of a dominant seventh chord in C major

If the seventh, which is F, moves down a step for the following chord it will be on E. If the augmented fourth B-F resolves by expanding to the nearest consonance it will become a sixth, E—C. What consonant triads in the key of C major would include C and E? Only the C major triad itself (I) or the A minor triad (vi).

So we see that adding a dissonant seventh to the dominant triad, V, can create an even stronger pull toward the I or vi chords for that key. We already knew that there is a very strong relationship between the tonic and dominant degrees of the scale, and now we have a way to alter the triad built on the dominant degree so that it will reinforce that relationship. The dominant seventh chord will seem to suggest to the ear that the next chord is going to be a tonic (or a vi, which can substitute for the tonic). The dominant seventh is a powerful means of telling the listener that a resolution to the tonic is about to happen, which is why it is unsettling if used as a final chord.

Building the dominant seventh in different keys

The dominant seventh chord is natural to all major keys. That means you don't need an accidental to write one if you are using the proper key signature: all four notes of the dominant seventh chord are unaltered scale notes as defined by the key signature of a major scale. Build a triad on the dominant degree of a scale and add a third; the third will automatically form the required minor third, which makes a minor seventh with the chord's root, which produces the dominant seventh:

Figure 7: Writing dominant sevenths in major keys

As we saw earlier, in minor keys the dominant chord requires an accidental to raise its third, producing a major triad with a leading tone to the tonic. Even here, though, once the chord is made major you have only to add a third without an accidental to make the dominant seventh chord:

Figure 8: Writing dominant sevenths in minor keys

Inversion of seventh chords

Adding a fourth note to the triad allows one more inversion. If the seventh itself is in the bass position the chord is in *third inversion*. A plain triad can't have a third inversion, of course.

C7   1st inversion 2nd inversion 3rd inversion

Figure 9: Close-position inversions of a seventh chord

Identifying chords quickly

It's a useful skill to be able to quickly identify the root and quality of a chord. This ability can, for example, enable you to recognize harmonies and create your own accompaniment. But the roots have gotten a little harder to recognize now that we have brought in seventh chords and inversions and doublings.

Here's a quick way to tell the root of any triadic chord (and not counting certain jazz chords): look for seconds, sevenths, perfect fourths and fifths.

If you see a second anywhere in the chord, then that is the inversion of a seventh, and so the chord must be a seventh chord and the upper note of the second must be its root:

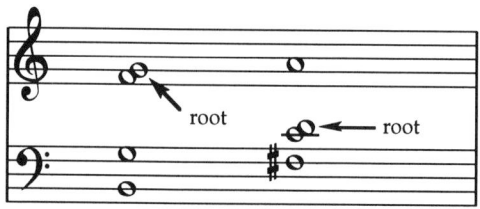

Figure 10: Using seconds to identify the root

You may see an uninverted seventh, in which case its lower note is the root:

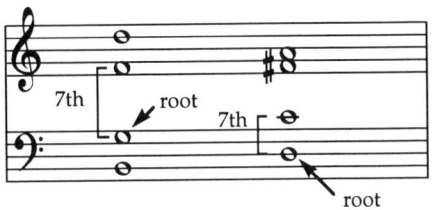

Figure 11: Using sevenths to identify the root

If you can see no seconds or sevenths (remember they may appear as compound intervals) then the chord must be a plain triad with perhaps some doubled notes. In that case the root will be the upper note of any perfect fourth you can find, or the lower note of any perfect fifth:

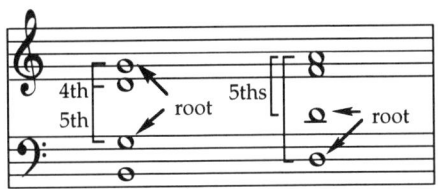

Figure 12: Using 4ths and 5ths to identify the root

 35

Activity

With Practica Musica in "practice mode" (not in any particular activity) enter a major triad whose root is G. Then add an F, anywhere above the root. How does Practica Musica describe the chord? Now turn off that F and enter it again *beneath* the root. What changed in the analysis by Practica Musica? Experiment by writing dominant seventh chords with different roots and in different inversions.

Other types of seventh chords

Adding a seventh to other types of triads can result in several distinct sonorities. In a major key the minor ii, iii, and vi triads will often have a minor seventh added, making a *minor seventh chord*. A vii° triad with a natural seventh (it always will come out to be a minor seventh) makes a *half-diminished seventh chord*, since the fifth is diminished but the seventh is not. If that seventh is lowered one half-step the result is a *diminished seventh chord*, which is made entirely of minor thirds, with the outer notes separated by a diminished seventh. Somewhat less common than any of these, at least in classical music, is the *major seventh chord*, which is obtained when a natural seventh is added to the I or IV chords in a major scale. All the same chords are produced in the minor keys, though they occur on different scale degrees.

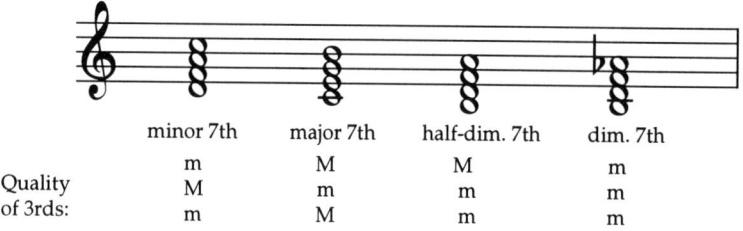

	minor 7th	major 7th	half-dim. 7th	dim. 7th
	m	M	M	m
Quality	M	m	m	m
of 3rds:	m	M	m	m

Figure 13: Examples of other seventh chords

The diminished seventh and half-diminished seventh

Of the above, the diminished seventh is the most unstable. Because it is so dissonant (it contains *two* diminished fifths within it and a diminished seventh as well) it has a strong sense of motion. Both it and the half-diminished seventh chord usually are built on the vii° triad and can be used more or less interchangeably with the dominant seventh (V7) chord; they resolve well to the tonic (the lowest three notes of the vii°7 are the same as the upper three notes of the V7). The only difference in function between the vii°7 chords and the dominant seventh is that the fully diminished vii°7 doesn't resolve well to vi, since its lowered seventh gives the impression of needing to resolve downward.

36

Activity

Select Chord Spelling from the Practica Musica Activities menu and attempt to pass Level 3. When you make mistakes be sure to look at the corrected chord that will appear to the right of your answer, and also read the analysis line to see what chord you actually did enter.

SUPPLEMENTARY TOPICS, CHAPTER XIII

Figured bass for seventh chords

As with the triads, numbers derived from figured bass often serve as abbreviations for the various inversions of seventh chords. "7" is the root position seventh chord, "6/5" means a first inversion seventh chord; "4/3" means the second inversion, and "4/2" means a third inversion. The figures again refer to intervals formed between the bass and the upper notes.

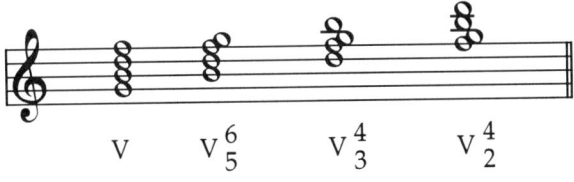

Figure 14: Figured bass labels for V7 chords

Ninth chords and beyond

If you continue to stack thirds on the basic triad you can produce chords that include ninths, elevenths, or even thirteenths. These sonorities are not really acknowledged as such in the classical music theory known to Mozart and Beethoven, though later composers and modern pop and jazz players like to use them explicitly. One reason classical tonal theory does not talk much about chords above the seventh is that it has other ways to refer to the same effects. A ninth, for example, may appear in a classical harmony but the composer probably did not consider it to be part of the chord — it was a dissonant tone outside the chord (this is the same way the "seventh chord" came into being, as a dissonance added to a triad). Or a composer might have created what looks to us like a full eleventh chord, but as far as the composer was concerned it was the dominant seventh chord being played at the same time as the tonic triad.

The main difference between the classical and modern use of such chords is that they are now often treated as sounds to be heard for their own sake rather than as dissonant preparations for consonant chords. So a jazz player, or a modern symphonist, does not necessarily resolve the seventh or the other dissonances as a classical musician would have done. On the other hand, jazz musicians are still likely to follow classical principles of voice-leading in other respects — keeping economy of motion, for example (see Chapter XIV).

The only simple guidelines that can be provided here for the use of chords beyond the seventh are these: they are usually played in root position, and if any notes must be left out you should at least include the root, the third, and the seventh. That is really just the same as classical practice, where the fifth is the most dispensible note in a chord. For example, a thirteenth chord could be voiced in four parts as follows:

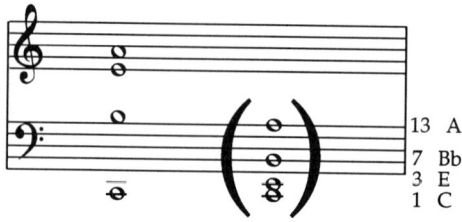

Figure 15: 13th chord voiced in 4 parts. () shows its notes in their original order.

Non-tertian harmonies

You should also be aware that modern composers sometimes construct *non-tertian harmonies* — chords built from intervals other than the third. These are not part of the language of classical tonal music, but you may like the sound of them. The most popular non-tertian harmonies are chords built of fourths and fifths, which are known respectively as *quartal* and *quintal* chords:

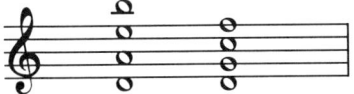

Figure 16: Quartal, quintal chords

Neither quartal nor quintal chords can invert without changing the nature of the harmony, since an inverted fourth is a fifth, and vice-versa. And it is not always easy to avoid the tertian sound: chords built of fifths may tend to sound like tertian harmonies with every other note missing. A quartal chord with only three notes may give the impression of being really a tertian chord with a raised third. To be perceived as what they are these non-tertian harmonies probably need to be placed in a context where the listener does not expect tertian harmonies.

Some musicians, such as the 20th-century composer Belà Bartok, have even built chords of major or minor seconds:

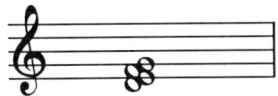

Figure 17: A chord built from seconds

After getting to know the traditional materials of harmony you may want to do some experimenting of your own.

Summary, Chapter XIII

1. Seventh chords are triads with another third added to the stack. Because the interval of a seventh is dissonant all types of seventh chords are unstable and were used in classical tonal music (the music of Mozart and Beethoven, for example) to give a sense of motion.

2. The dominant seventh is the most common type of seventh chord, formed by adding a minor seventh to the dominant triad.

3. Seventh chords have one more possible inversion: if the seventh itself is in the bass the chord is in the *third inversion*.

4. To quickly identify the root of an unknown chord, look first for any seconds or sevenths. If you see either one (they may be compound) the chord is a seventh chord and its root is the upper note of the second or the lower note of the seventh. If there are no seconds or sevenths in the chord, again including compound ones, then look for fifths or fourths: the upper note of the fourth or the lower note of the fifth will be the root.

5. Other types of seventh chord are the minor seventh chord (a minor seventh added to the ii, iii, vi chords), the half-diminished seventh (a seventh chord built from the vii° chord), the fully-diminished seventh (usually made from the vii° also, but requiring an accidental), and the major seventh, such as is formed by adding a natural seventh to the I or the IV.

Supplementary topics

6. "7," "6/5," "4/3," and "4/2" are the figured bass terms for the root position, first, second, and third inversions of a seventh chord.

7. Triadic harmonies can also be formed that include 9ths, 11ths, or 13ths. These are used in jazz, but they are not an explicit part of classical theory. Some notes can be left out of these chords: the most important ones to keep are the root, third, and seventh.

8. Chords can also be built from intervals other than the third, though such harmonies are not part of the language of tonal music. The most common of these *non-tertian* harmonies are *quartal* and *quintal* chords (chords built from stacked fourths or fifths).

XIV. VOICE-LEADING

Classical harmony, which has much in common with modern popular harmony, is typically conceived in several simultaneous parts — as if it were being sung by three or four voices or played by a quartet of strings. So it is helpful to think of harmony not as a series of chords but as several lines of melody that form chords between them as they move. Generally the best results are obtained when each of those melodies is graceful in itself and cooperates well with the others without losing its independence. Musicians have evolved a number of effective techniques to attain these goals, which we study as the art of *voice-leading*.

In the below example four voices combine to form a series of chords. The voices are first written on separate staves so that you can easily see the melody of each one, and then they are combined on a single grand staff, as they probably would appear in sheet music. On each quarter note (every beat) a new chord is formed by the combined voices (the eighth-notes in between the beats aren't part of the chords, as we'll see later). The music is from a chorale for four voices by J.S. Bach, *Herzlich lieb hab ich dich, o Herr* :

Figure 1: Four-voice harmony, separately

Figure 2: Four-voice harmony, combined on a grand staff

The chords formed by the voices of that chorale are easier to recognize if separated from the non-chordal tones:

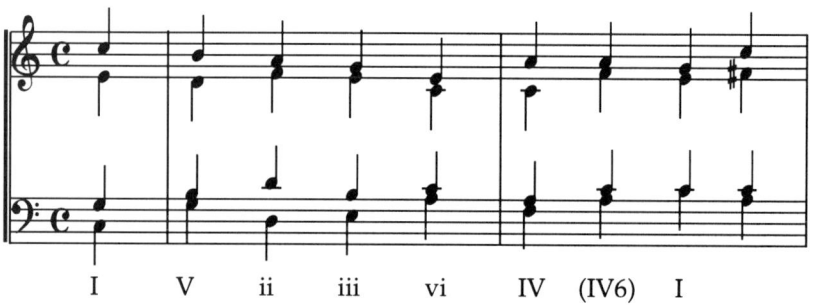

I   V   ii   iii   vi   IV   (IV6)   I

Figure 2a: Chords extracted from Figure 2

Keyboard music can often work in a similar way, even if the "voices" are not so clear. The broken chords in the bass clef part of this piano sonata can be simplified to show that they are basically three-voice harmony. Add the treble-clef melody and we again have four voices:

Figure 3: "Voices" in keyboard music (from Mozart's Sonata in C)

Principles of voice-leading

Successful voice-leading in tonal music depends on three things: a good melody for each voice, sufficient independence for each voice, and resolution of any dissonances formed between the voices. Each of these will be treated in more detail below.

Economy of motion

When making a chord change it's often helpful to voice the second chord in such a way as to minimize the amount of movement required by each voice. This tends to result in smoother melodies within the harmony.

For example, if the new chord has notes in common with the preceding one, then perhaps those notes should just be repeated in the same voice. Perhaps you can arrange things so that none of the voices needs to move more than a second in order to reach the notes of the new harmony, as in this example:

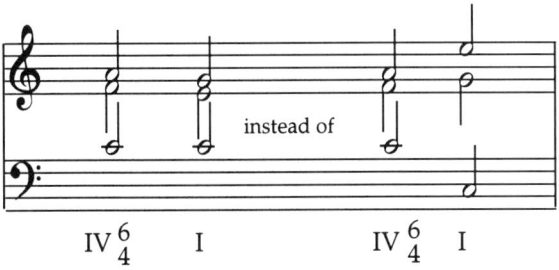

Figure 4: Economy of motion in chord changes

The principle of *economy of motion*, which helps to achieve smooth and connected melodic lines, is one that is valid in modern jazz and pop as well as in the classical style.

Independence of voices

The relative motion of a pair of voices can be *similar,   parallel,
contrary,* or *oblique*:

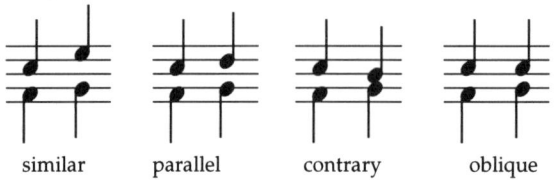

Figure 5: Different kinds of relative motion

The types of motion that produce the greatest sense of independence are, of course, contrary and oblique motion, and then similar
motion. Parallel motion is frequently used in harmony, but mostly using
the weaker consonant intervals like the third and sixth, as in this example:

Land where my   fa- thers died, land of the   pil- grims' pride,

Figure 6: Parallel thirds

Parallel motion at the strong perfect intervals of the fifth or the octave is
avoided in classical tonal harmony because it seems to reduce the independence of voices. Most classical writers were careful to avoid even a
single parallel fifth or octave; they would probably not have written the
below example, which contains parallel perfect intervals (marked with
heavy lines):

Figure 7: Undesirable parallel octaves and fifths

Fourths are perfect intervals, but since they are not as strong as fifths and octaves they are sometimes written in parallel, especially if combined with thirds:

Figure 8: Acceptable parallel fourths

Avoidance of parallel perfect intervals is a part of the classical style but not necessarily of modern music. Nonetheless, you should be aware of parallels, and practicing to avoid them helps you acquire skill.

Dissonance handling

A composition would be a dull thing if it contained only consonant harmonies. Most pieces employ frequent dissonances. In classical tonal harmony, however, close attention is paid to how dissonances are *approached* and how they are *resolved* to a consonance. For our purposes it will be enough to state just two basic principles for handling dissonances:

1) A dissonance should be resolved to a consonance before proceding to another dissonance (don't write two dissonant notes in a row).

2) A dissonance is usually approached by step and almost always is resolved by step. Sometimes it can be approached by leap, if it is resolved by step in the opposite direction.

Most dissonances that you will encounter in tonal music are treated according to these principles. All of the dissonant notes in the Bach chorale of Figure 2, for example, are approached by step and then immediately resolved by step. Here is that example again, this time with the dissonant notes circled:

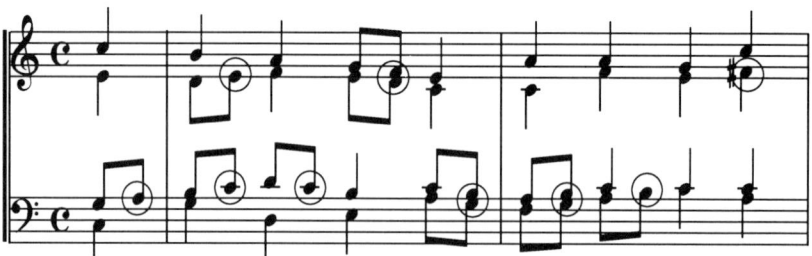

Figure 9: Dissonances in the earlier example from Bach

Accented vs. unaccented dissonances

All but one of the above dissonances occur in rhythmically weak (unaccented or offbeat) positions. Only one accented dissonance appears, the F# on the last beat of the second measure. The distinction between accented and unaccented dissonances is useful because you will need to be more strict in the treatment of accented dissonances. Unaccented dissonances will occasionally leap to a resolution but accented ones almost always resolve by step.

Some practice writing in the chorale style

A good way to practice voice-leading is to write a four-voice chorale in which the harmony changes with every beat. Like the Bach example above, a chorale is a song for soprano, alto, tenor, and bass, and it is usually written on two staves with the note stems alternating in direction so that the voices will be clearly separated. To start with we'll just write four simple chords without separating the voices:

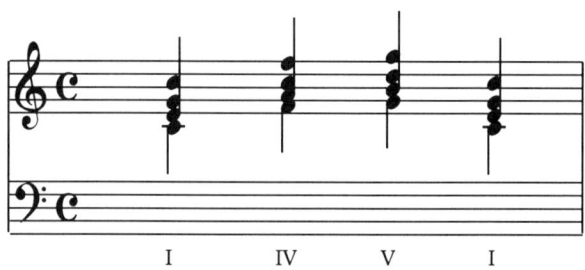

     I   IV   V   I

Figure 10: The chords I, IV, V, I, in close root position

These chords are all moving parallel, and so the harmony is full of parallel fifths and octaves. It would be better if each of the parts had some degree of independence, which we can obtain by *revoicing* the chords (rearranging their notes):

Figure 11: The same chords, revoiced

Now each voice has a melody different from the others, and though the harmonies are exactly the same the composition is more interesting. You can see how chord inversions arise; we put the IV chord in first inversion to make a descending bass line on beat two. The other chords are still in root position, but they have been spread out into open voicing and the upper notes of each chord are in a different order. We've also avoided getting either very high or very low, since the traditional ideal for part-writing is the vocal quartet of soprano, alto, tenor, and bass.

However, we've still used only the same notes that we started with, all of which form consonant harmonies. A few added dissonances would add both interest and movement. In places where a voice leaps by a third we could sometimes insert an unaccented dissonant note that is approached by step and resolved by step, as follows:

Figure 12 : Adding unaccented dissonances

An accented dissonance would add a little drama to the next-to-last chord. Just find a note a step above one of the chord tones, play that note on the beat, and then resolve to the chord tone, as follows:

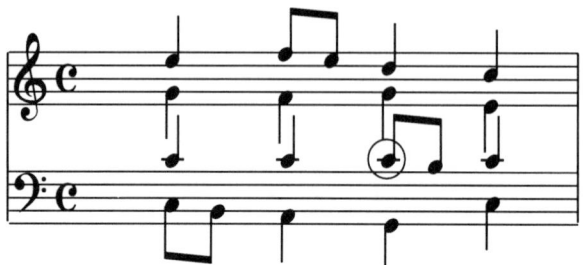

Figure 13: Adding an accented dissonance (circled)

These would work, too:

Figure 14: Some other accented dissonances for beat three

Simple as it is, this four measure composition is certainly a great advance over the plain chords! And though it is written in a style modeled after that of Bach, the voice-leading principles involved are also useful in other types of music.

SUPPLEMENTARY TOPICS, CHAPTER XIV

The *non-chordal tones* mentioned above and in Chapter X can be classified into several common types, which are found in both classical and popular music. Knowing these typical non-chordal tones will help you to handle dissonances gracefully when writing music in several parts.

The passing tone

When a melodic line moving stepwise departs just briefly from consonance to "pass through" a dissonant interval we call the dissonant note a *passing tone*. These are usually unaccented but can be placed on the beat. In these examples the dissonant passing tones are circled, and the notes that follow them are the consonant notes that resolve the dissonance.

accented
passing tones

unaccented
passing tones

Figure 15: Accented and unaccented passing tones

Passing tones are by far the most common type of dissonance. If you look again at the Bach chorale in Figure 10, you'll see that every dissonance in it can be described as a passing tone, even the F# in the last chord of measure two.

The neighboring tone

The neighboring tone is like a passing tone, but it comes back to where it started instead of going on, as follows:

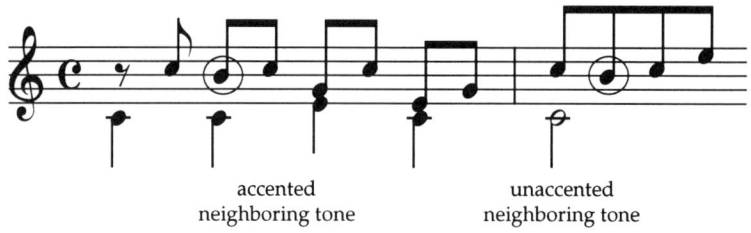

accented
neighboring tone

unaccented
neighboring tone

Figure 16: Accented and unaccented neighboring tones

The appoggiatura

The *appoggiatura* is an accented dissonance that is approached by leap and which then moves by step to a consonant interval. The leap is usually upwards and the resolution usually downwards:

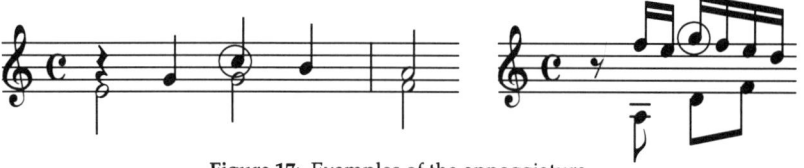

Figure 17: Examples of the appoggiatura

The suspension

In the *suspension* a held or repeated note becomes dissonant at an accented position because its accompanying chordal tones have changed, and then it moves by step to agree with the others. As with the appoggiatura, its resolution is usually downward. In the example below the tied note is a suspension; it becomes dissonant with the accompaniment on beat three. This suspension could just as easily have been written with a halfnote instead of the two tied quarters.

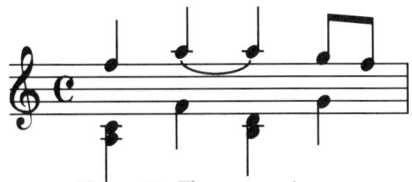

Figure 18: The suspension

Bach chorales are rich sources for illustrations of voice-leading practice. This one, *Herzlich thut mich verlangen*, includes two suspensions of the repeated-note type, which are in the alto voice (the next-highest) on beat four of measure 1 and beat 1 of measure 2.

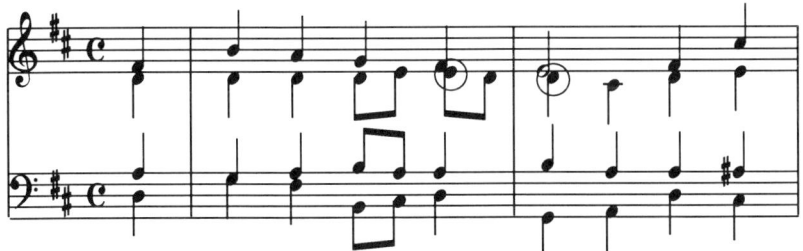

Figure 19: Suspensions in a Bach chorale (circled)

Notice in both chorale examples how Bach is careful to avoid parallel fifths or octaves. You can examine his work by finding every fifth or octave in the harmony and then checking the relative motion of the voices as they move to the following interval. The motion is almost always contrary or oblique, as in the pickup to measure 1:

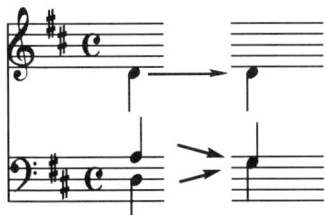

Figure 20: Bach's avoidance of parallel fifths and octaves

The avoidance of parallel perfect intervals is mostly important for music that has a set number of voices, such as vocal music or music for several melody instruments. But even in classical piano music we can often see some evidence of the voice-leading principles, as in the below example from Mozart, the same sonata that was quoted in Figure 2. The dissonances in these three measures are a little harder to recognize than those of the Bach because the Alberti bass breaks up the chords:

Figure 21: Mozart: *Sonata in C,* first three measures
(available for listening in "Chapter 10, Figure 03")

We can get a clearer picture of Mozart's harmonies if we again condense these broken chords to a simpler form:

Figure 22: Harmonies condensed from Mozart's sonata

Most of the dissonance in this excerpt is in measure two. The F in the first chord of measure two is an accented neighboring tone that resolves by downward step to an E in the second chord of that measure. The D beneath it could also be called an accented neighboring tone if we consider this fourth to be dissonant, as Mozart probably did (the fourth is usually considered dissonant if one of its notes is the bass). The C in the right hand (upper voice) is also a dissonance in that G major triad, but it is a passing tone that resolves by step to a consonant D. The F on the first beat of the third measure is another technically-dissonant fourth that resolves downward by step.

Though the music of Bach and Mozart seems most of the time to "follow the rules" of dissonance handling and voice leading that is not to say that either composer was restricted in any way. For Mozart, as with J.S. Bach, musical technique came from personal taste rather than a "following of rules." That is, both composers learned various rules as the means of writing what they wanted to write. Neither would have considered these rules to be an infringement of their freedom — they were, and are, just a way to achieve a desired result.

Summary, Chapter XIV

1. Classical harmony is typically conceived in several simultaneous parts; it is helpful sometimes to think of harmony not as a series of chords but rather as several simultaneous melodies.

2. Voice-leading is the art of making several melodies work gracefully together to make harmonic changes.

3. Successful voice-leading depends on a good melody for each voice, sufficient independence for each voice, and resolution of any dissonances formed between the voices.

4. Voice-leading benefits from *economy of motion*: when changing chords the movement between voices should be minimized. Each voice should, if possible, move to the nearest available tone of the next chord.

5. The relative motion of a pair of voices can be *parallel* or *similar, contrary,* or *oblique*. Parallel motion at the perfect fifth and octave should be avoided in the classical style.

6. Parallel fourths are less objectionable than parallel fifths, especially when combined with thirds.

7. Rules for dissonances:

1) A dissonance should be resolved to a consonance before proceeding to another dissonance (don't write two dissonant notes in a row).

2) A dissonance is usually approached by step and almost always is resolved by step. Sometimes it can be approached by leap, if it is resolved by step in the opposite direction.

Supplementary topics

8. The *non-chordal tones* are standard ways of treating dissonances. The most common types are the *passing tone,* the *neighbor tone,* the *appoggiatura,* and the *suspension.*

APPENDICES

The physics of music

All sound is vibration, but the pitched sounds used in music are vibrations at a constant rate per second, called the *frequency of vibration*. For most people's ears the lowest frequency that sounds like a musical tone is about 27 vibrations per second, about that produced by the lowest note on a full-sized piano. The highest frequency we can hear diminishes as we grow older but at its best rarely exceeds 16,000 cycles per second, about two octaves above the highest note of a piano. The ability to hear high pitches (or, as we'll see below, the high components of lower notes) is permanently damaged by exposure to loud sounds, something that should be borne in mind when attending amplified concerts.

Since sound vibration amounts to a fluctuation in air pressure it is often represented in two-dimensional graphic form with time running on the horizontal axis and pressure on the vertical axis:

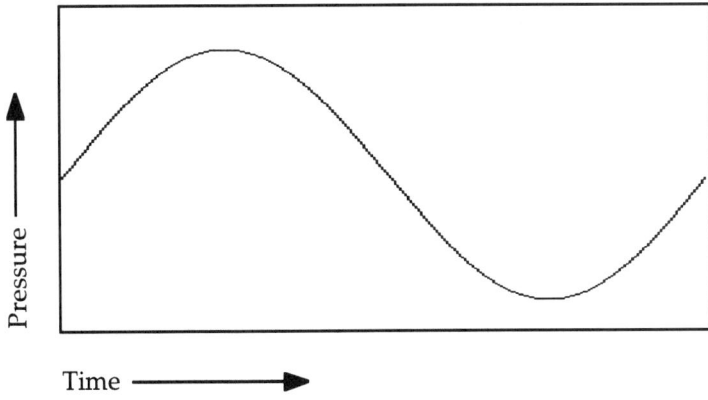

Figure 1: Graph of a sound wave

The above graph shows a smooth increase and decrease in pressure which, if repeated 110 times a second, would sound like a very colorless "A" two octaves below middle C. This simple curve follows the shape of the mathmatical sine function, and so it is called a *sine wave*. However, sounds created by acoustic (i.e., not electronic) musical instruments are never so plain as this, because any physical object is too complicated to produce only a sine wave when it vibrates. For example, here is the waveform of part of a note played by a trumpet:

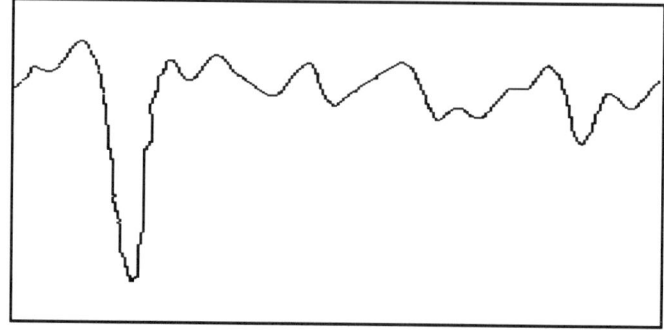

Figure 2: Waveform from an acoustic musical instrument

The trumpet waveform can actually be analyzed as the sum of many sine waves of different frequency, all of which are being heard simultaneously. That's why natural sounds are said to be *complex*; they are a mixture of many different frequencies.

In musical sounds these different frequency components have an interesting relationship to each other which can be illustrated by examining a hypothetical vibrating string.

If you pluck a string that is tightly stretched between two points it will vibrate along its whole length, creating a waveform like the sine wave above, but it will also vibrate in halves, thirds, fourths, fifths, etc. The figure below illustrates, in a very exaggerated way, the first three modes of vibration of a taut string:

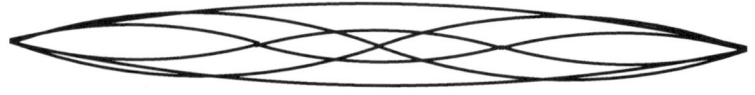

Figure 3: Three modes of vibration of a taut string

The various modes of vibration give rise to the additional tones that complicate the wave form graph. Ideally (if the string is perfectly flexible and even) each of these other tones has a frequency closely related to the original one produced by the whole string. If the whole string is vibrating at 110 cycles per second, half if it will vibrate at twice 110, or 220, a third of it will vibrate at three times 110, and so on. Each of these other vibrations will sound like a note, so that the sound of the whole vibrating string is actually a combination of many pitches. If you listen very carefully to a vibrating guitar string, you can actually hear the other tones, which are known as *partials* or *overtones*. For example, if you played a low "A" you would hear these partials:

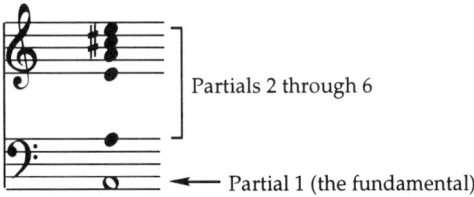

Partials 2 through 6

Partial 1 (the fundamental)

Figure 4: Overtone series for A

Since the same phenomenon occurs with columns of air, as in the trumpet, and in fact any vibrating body, the overtone series is part of all musical sounds. In some instruments, like bells, the overtones are distorted by the stiffness of the material, but most pitched instruments make a fairly accurate overtone series at least as high as we can hear it (theoretically it goes on forever). This brings us to the importance of the overtone series for harmony.

If you play two notes at the same time they will each have their own overtone series, and if the two notes happen to have just the right relationship to each other some of those overtones may match or come close to matching. For example, suppose you play A and E together:

Figure 5: Matched overtones in a fifth

If the shared overtones *almost* match, an interference pattern is created that sounds like a wavering or *beating*. You can, however, carefully raise or lower the pitch of one of the notes until the beating stops, which will happen when the coincident overtones match exactly. At that point the two notes will seem to be in "agreement." We could also say that they are "in tune."

It is difficult to hear overtones beyond the first six or so, since they become faint, but the first six are enough. The sixth is a convenient place to stop for other reasons as well: the seventh partial would create an interval that had no possibility of agreement with any of the first six, and the eighth partial is merely an octave, so the next practical partial is the ninth, which is so quiet that it can't affect harmony very much. The possibilities for matching between the first six partials give us all of the musical intervals that we say have the potential, if adjusted carefully, of being in agreement or being "consonant." In fact, our ear accepts these as being basically in agreement even if they are slightly out-of tune; the limit of our tolerance seems to be that amount of distuning that would make the beats come too quickly to easily counted. However, not all intervals have this potential for consonance, because not all of them have matches among the most easily-heard partials. The intervals with a clear potential for agreement are the unison, octave, fifth, fourth, major and minor thirds, and major and minor sixths. The other intervals, such as the second, have no possibility of matched partials among the first six, and so we regard them as being comparatively unrelated, unstable, or "dissonant."

---

37   **Activity**

If you are using one of the standard built-in Practica Musica instruments (piano. guitar, organ, or voice) you can try this experiment: select Temperament from the Sound Options menu and choose the "Just" tuning. Now play the C major triad again and listen very carefully, preferably with a set of headphones. The "just" tuning allows you to hear the C major triad in its theoretically perfect form, with each note smoothly agreeing with the other. The effect is particularly noticeable with the organ and the harpsichord. Contrast the sound of the just triad with that of a Pythagorean one, which has a third that is considerably sharper than just. Once you can hear that distinction, compare the just triad to that of equal temperament, where the third is about half that sharp.

Instrumental color

Different musical instruments give varying emphasis to each of the partials, which accounts for a large part of each instrument's characteristic "color." The clarinet, for example, emphasizes just the odd-numbered partials, whereas the oboe is rich in all of them. The highest partials of the piano are quieter than those of the harpsichord, and they are also more distorted, since the strings of the piano are thicker in relation to their length. The improved sound of a full-size grand piano is largely owing to the longer and relatively thinner strings, which allow more accurate partials and clearer tone.

Changes in partials are also an important part of instrument color: plucked strings like those of the guitar begin with many partials and lose the higher ones as the sound dies away; a trumpet note, conversely, can begin with relatively few partials and gain more as it progresses.

Extraneous noises are significant for some instruments, though we may notice them only when they are missing. These include the wind or "chiff" at the beginning of a note played by a large organ pipe, the thunk of a piano hammer against the string, and the scraping sounds produced by a violin bow as it attempts to start a string moving. There are also various other tones that come from the resonance of other parts of the instrument: the tone of the various wood parts of a violin mixes with the tone produced by the bowed string, for example. The result is that the sound of an acoustic instrument can be extremely complex, which is why it is so difficult to imitate electronically.

Temperament

You would think that the ideal way to tune your piano would be to make each of the consonant intervals sound exactly in tune, so that no beating could be heard. Indeed, many musicians have long regarded this as a sort of ideal, but it doesn't work out very well on a keyboard with only twelve keys to the octave. For example, you can tune your A so that it will make a very nice sixth above your C, and the G as a good fifth above the C and the D to make a good fifth below A, but then you'll find that the G will be out of tune with the D. In other words, it doesn't come out even;

you can't tune all the consonances to be simultaneously exactly right unless you have two different keys for some of the notes, such as one D tuned to agree with G and another D made to work with A.

This problem was solved in many different ways over the years. The first solution was to tune the fifths exactly right and not to worry about the thirds and sixths, just as Pythagorus, the semi-legendary discoverer of musical mathematics, had done. This *Pythagorean* tuning was the basis of organ tuning and music theory until around the late 14th or early 15th century, which is why thirds and sixths were regarded before that time as dissonant intervals.

But when musicians began to want to use the consonant third a compromise had to be found, and they responded by tuning that troublesome D to the *mean* (average) of the two that were needed, which produced a system in which *most* of the thirds were very good and *most* of the fifths were only slightly off; this we now call *meantone temperament* (to "temper" an interval means to adjust its tuning a little bit away from perfect).

Meantone was used for several centuries and is still enjoyed by connoisseurs of early music, but it had one problem: since four of the less-common thirds were very discordant (and one fifth, the *wolf fifth*, was really awful), meantone didn't allow the free use of all the intervals in all the keys. So musicians began to alter the compromise a little with the hope of making the wolf and the bad thirds less objectionable. The *Silbermann* temperament is a variation of meantone in which the wolf is gone, the bad thirds are not quite so large, and the good thirds are, in trade, not quite so good as they were in normal meantone. Other people invented schemes in which some chords have both perfect thirds and perfect fifths and others have varying shades of inexactness; the *Kirnberger* tempera-ment is an example. In these tunings that grew out of meantone there begins to be some variety in the quality of the acceptable chords, which may have contributed to the notion that different keys have different characters — for example, C major was thought to be pure and cheerful, while F# major was harsh and dark.

The temperament that won out in the end, at least so far, was *equal temperament*, in which all the thirds are just barely OK but all the fifths are very good. Equal temperament has much to recommend it;

besides being the same in all keys its large major thirds are well-suited to melody, which is an important factor in our music. For some reason musicians often prefer large thirds for melody even though the smaller thirds make smoother harmony. Fortunately, most of us are able to accept the larger thirds in harmony, too, especially since the modern piano does not emphasize the higher overtones the way the harpsichord did. Nonetheless, many musicians experiment with tuning, and there may yet be something of a revival of alternate systems, even ones with more than 12 notes to the octave, which are much easier to implement with electronic musical instruments than they were with mechanical ones.

Following is a chart of the each of the tunings and temperaments provided with *Practica Musica*. The variations in tuning are measured in *cents* (one cent = 1/1200 octave or 1/100 of an equal-tempered halfstep). The upper rows show the size of the major third above each note, as compared with the acoustically exact interval, and the lower rows show the same comparison for the fifth above the given note. A zero in either place means that the interval is acoustically exact and will sound without any 'beating.'

Equal temperament

14	14	14	14	14	14	14	14	14	14	14	14
F	C	G	D	A	E	B	F#	C#	G#	D#	A#
-2	-2	-2	-2	-2	-2	-2	-2	-2	-2	-2	-2

Pythagorean

22	22	22	-2	-2	-2	-2	22	22	22	22	22
F	C	G	D	A	E	B	Gb	Db	Ab	Eb	Bb
0	0	0	0	0	0	-24	0	0	0	0	0

Meantone

0	0	0	0	0	0	42	42	42	42	0	0
F	C	G	D	A	E	B	F#	C#	G#	Eb	Bb
-5.5	-5.5	-5.5	-5.5	-5.5	-5.5	-5.5	-5.5	-5.5	37	-5.5	-5.5

Silbermann 1/6 comma

6	6	6	10	14	18	22	22	22	18	14	10
F	C	G	D	A	E	B	F#	C#	G#	Eb	Bb
-4	-4	-4	-4	-4	-4	0	0	0	0	0	0

Kirnberger 1/2 comma

F	C	G	D	A	E	B	F#	C#	G#	Eb	Bb
0	0	0	9	20	20	20	22	22	22	22	9
0	0	0	-11	-11	0	0	0	0	0	0	0

Tempérament ordinaire

F	C	G	D	A	E	B	F#	C#	G#	Eb	Bb
8.5	0	2.5	5	5.5	10	15	20	29	32	24.5	17
3	-5.5	-5.5	-5.5	-5.5	-3	-3	-6	0	2	2	3

Just scale in C

F	C	G	D	A	E	B	F#	C#	G#	Eb	Bb
0	0	0	0	22	22	20	20	20	20	22	22
0	0	0	-22	0	0	0	0	0	-2	0	0

Extended meantone

Divides the octave into 35 notes without enharmonic equivalents, where every major third is exactly tuned and every perfect fifth is 5 1/2 cents flat.

Extended Pythagorean

Divides the octave into 35 notes without enharmonic equivalents, where every major third is 22 cents wide and every perfect fifth is exact.

Glossary

Aeolian mode. The mode or scale represented by the piano's white keys beginning with A. Equivalent to the modern *natural minor*.

accent. 1) An expression mark, $>$, that calls for emphasis on a note.
2) Metric accent: An accented note is one in a strong rhythmic position: on a beat or on a duple subdivision of a beat (such as the first or third of a group of four 16th notes).

accidental. A sign used to raise or lower a note without changing its letter name. There are five accidental signs: ♯ ♭ ♮ 𝄪 𝄫

anacrusis. Unaccented (upbeat) notes at the beginning of a phrase. The tune "The Itsy-Bitsy Spider" begins with an anacrusis (p. 44).

arpeggio. A chord played one-note-after-another, as on a harp.

asymmetrical meter. A meter that is divisible by neither three nor two: e.g., 5/4, 7/8, etc.

augmented. Enlarged one semitone beyond major or perfect.

augmented sixth. A sixth that is one semitone larger than a major sixth.

augmented sixth chords. These come about when a composer about to reach a dominant harmony decides to use dissonances in the voice-leading that would approach the root of a dominant chord by halfstep from both sides at once. The sixth scale degree is lowered, bringing it to within a halfstep of the dominant from the upper side, and the fourth degree is raised. The resulting interval of an augmented sixth gives this effect its name. Depending on what other notes are used in addition to the augmented sixth itself, the result will be either the "French," the "Italian," or the "German" augmented sixth chords, or else one that is called the "doubly-augmented fourth." Below are examples with typical resolutions:

Ger. 6+,V   Fr. 6+,V   It. 6+, V   4++6+, I$^6_4$

bass. The lowest note in a chord or interval.

beat. The steady (and silent) pulse that underlies measured music.

beam. A slanted or horizontal bar that connects two or more note stems as a replacement for the *flag*.

chord. Any simultaneous combination of more than two pitch classes.

consonance. An interval or chord is generally said to be consonant if its notes share one or more of the more easily heard overtones (the lower overtones are the easiest to hear). The shared overtones lend a sense of stability to the combination. The consonances in order of stability are the unison, octave, fifth, fourth (which, however is considered dissonant under some circumstances - see *dissonance*), major third, minor third, major sixth, and minor sixth. "Consonance" is a relative term, as is "dissonance."

chromatic. See *genera*.

compound meter. A meter in which the beat is represented by a dotted note; e.g. 3/8, 6/8, 9/8, 12/8 (respectively 1, 2, 3, or 4 beats/ measure).

crescendo. Getting louder.

da capo. Italian "from the beginning." Abbrev. "D.C."

da capo al fine. Italian "from the beginning to the marked *fine* (end)." Abbrev. "D.C. al fine"

dal segno al fine. Italian "from the sign to the marked *fine* (end)." Abbrev. "D.S. al fine."

decrescendo. Getting quieter.

diatonic. See *genera*.

dissonance. An interval that is not acoustically stable, or which is treated as such in traditional music theory. Dissonant intervals are the seconds, sevenths, all augmented or diminished intervals, and the fourth when alone or involving the bass. See *consonance*.

dominant. The fifth degree of the scale, or the chord built on the fifth degree of the scale.

dominant seventh. A major chord with a minor seventh. In a major key it occurs naturally only on the fifth, or dominant, degree of the scale — hence the name.

Dorian. The medieval mode beginning on D, same pattern as the white keys starting on D.

dotted note. A note followed by a dot, which increases the note value by half and therefore makes the note a triple quantity rather than a duple one. Example: a dotted quarternote equals three eighth-notes.

double-flat. ♭♭ Lowers a note by two semitones.

double-sharp. ✗ Raises a note by two semitones.

doubling. Repeating one of the pitch classes in a chord.

duple. Capable of being divided evenly by two.

dynamics. Loudness or softness.

enharmonic. Two notes, intervals, or chords are enharmonic with each other if they are spelled differently but sound the same on the piano. Examples: F# and Gb, major third and diminished fourth, German augmented sixth chord and dominant seventh chord. See *genera*.

fifth. The fifth note of the scale or an interval comprising five scale steps.

figured bass. (thoroughbass) The practice of writing numbers under the bass notes to indicate harmonies.

first inversion. A chord is in first inversion if its third is in the bass position.

flag. On a note stem, the descending or rising extension used for notes shorter than a quarternote. See *beam*.

flat. The sign, ♭, which lowers a note one semitone.

fourth. The fourth degree of a scale, or the interval that covers four scale steps.

genera. The ancient Greek genera were three ways of building a four-note scale within the space of a fourth. The *diatonic* genus broke the fourth up into two wholesteps (tones) and a halfstep. A more unusual division was the *chromatic*, which consisted of two halfsteps of different size and a minor third. The last and most exotic was the *enharmonic*: a major third, a halfstep, and a tiny interval (smaller than a halfstep), called a *diesis*. All these words continue to have meanings based on their original significance to the Greeks. *Diatonic* music is music based on major or minor scales or the medieval modes; all of which are called diatonic because they resemble the diatonic genus above — they employ wholetones and that type of halfstep in which the note-name changes. *Chromatic* music involves at least some halfsteps in which the note name remains the same, as in the chromatic genus. Similarly, the word *enharmonic* still refers to the relationship between two notes that are written differently and would in theory be separated by a *diesis*, and yet are played on the same key of the piano, such as E# and F. Below is an attempt to represent the genera in modern notation:

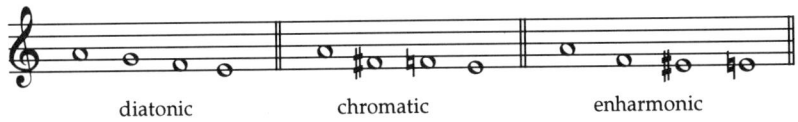

diatonic   chromatic   enharmonic

half-diminished. Describes the type of seventh chord in which the fifth is diminished but the seventh is not. Ex.: BDFA

hemiola. A special type of syncopation in which a duple pair is played in the time of a triple group, or vice-versa. Example: a pair of dotted eighth-notes in 3/8 meter.

Ionian. The mode beginning on C. Equivalent to the modern major scale.

interval. The difference in pitch between two notes; the combination of the two.

intonation. The exact pitch. The violin and the voice are examples of instruments capable of *free intonation*, because they can adjust the pitch in increments smaller than a semitone. Keyboard instruments have *fixed intonation*.

inversion. An interval or chord can be inverted, exchanging the relative positions of its notes. C-E is the inversion of E-C.

key. 1) The scale being used, as in the *key* of D. 2) One of the claves, or levers, of the keyboard.

key signature. At the beginning of each staff, the flats or sharps needed for the key are arranged in a key signature.

leading tone. 1) The seventh scale degree in a major, harmonic minor, or melodic minor scale 2) Any note that is a half-step away from its apparent destination.

Lydian. The medieval mode beginning on F; same pattern as the white keys starting on F.

mediant. The third note of a scale or the chord built on it.

Mixolydian. The medieval mode beginning on G; same pattern as the white keys starting on G.

major. 1) The larger of the two forms of the second, seventh, third, or sixth.

2) Also used to describe a scale or chord whose first third is major.

meter. The beat-grouping of a piece: 3/4, 4/4, etc.

minor. 1) The smaller of the two forms of the second, seventh, third, or sixth. 2) Also used to describe a scale or chord whose first third is minor.

mode. Essentially equivalent to *scale*. Commonly used to refer to the medieval modes *Dorian, Phrygian, Lydian,* and *Mixolydian,* or any diatonic scales other than standard major and minor.

natural. 1) Unaltered and played on the white keys of the piano.

2) The accidental sign, ♮, used to naturalize a note.

natural minor. The type of minor scale formed by the white keys starting on A.

octatonic scale. An eight-tone scale that consists of alternating half steps and whole steps. It is not a traditional scale, but was used by some 19th-century Russian composers and by Igor Stravinski, a 20th-century composer who came from that school. Example:

octave. The interval between any note and the next one bearing the same name; e.g., C to C. More precisely, a *perfect octave* is the interval between two notes that have exactly the same name (the pitch of one is exactly twice that of the other). C to C# would be an *augmented* octave; C to Cb a *diminished* octave.

overtone. Also called a *partial*. Any musical tone is actually a complex of many *partials* in which the frequency of the most audible partials is approximately an integer multiple of the starting, or *fundamental*, frequency.

perfect. Describes a unison, octave, fifth, or fourth that is neither diminished nor augmented.

pitch. The perceived "highness" or "lowness" of a note.

pitch class. Two notes have the same "pitch class" if their name is exactly the same (i.e., they are separated by one or more perfect octaves).

Phrygian. The medieval mode beginning on E; same pattern as the white keys starting on E.

Pythagorean. Following the principles of Pythagoras, the semi-legendary Greek founder of the science of harmony. Specifically refers to a scale tuning in which all notes are derived by tuning a series of acoustically exact fifths.

resolve. A dissonant interval generally resolves to a consonant one in classical tonal music, dissipating what is meant to be perceived as the tension of the dissonance.

root position. A chord is in root position if its root is also its bass.

scale. Any pattern of steps that fills in the space of an octave and which may be regarded as raw material for a piece of music. Scales were actually invented by theorists, who derived them from existing melodies.

second. Any interval covering two letter names, such as C-D or C# - D.

second inversion. A chord is in second inversion if its fifth is in the bass.

semitone. The smallest interval available on a standard keyboard; half of a wholetone.

seventh. An interval covering seven letter names.

sharp. A sign, ♯, used to raise a note by one semitone.

sixth. The interval of a sixth, covering 6 letter names.

solfege. Vocal exercise using the solmization syllables.

solmization. The use of the syllables "do, re, mi..." to remember the sound of the major or minor scales.

staff. The five horizontal lines on which notes are written in *staff notation*.

subdominant. The fourth scale degree, or a chord built on that degree.

submediant. The sixth scale degree, or a chord built on it.

subtonic. The seventh scale degree. Usually called this only if it is a wholetone away from the tonic. If it is just a semitone from the tonic the seventh degree is called the *leading tone.*

supertonic. The second scale degree, or a chord built on it.

syncopation. In rhythm, a pattern that emphasizes the off-beats, usually by beginning notes on an offbeat and holding them over through the start of a beat.

temperament. If intervals are tuned acoustically exact they don't come out "even" with only twelve keys on the keyboard. Temperament systems make various compromises with acoustical exactitude for the sake of practicality. Equal temperament is the modern standard, in which all the major thirds are somewhat wide of their acoustically exact size and all the fifths are very slightly narrow.

tonal. Tonal music is based on the notes of a single diatonic scale, in which the tonic has the most important role. Both classical and popular music are tonal.

tonic. The first note of a diatonic scale.

transpose. To raise or lower the pitch of a passage, as in transposing a song from C major to D major.

triad. A group of three notes, the pitch classes of which are separated by thirds, such as C,E,G.

triple. Capable of being divided evenly by three.

triplet. Rhythmically, three in the time of two.

unison. The interval composed of two notes having the same letter name and written on the same line or space. May be perfect, augmented, or diminished.

voicing. The spacing, doubling, and arrangement of the notes of a chord. Voicing may be altered without changing the harmony.

wholenote. The basic unit of rhythm in notation. Equal to 4 quarternotes, 8 eighthnotes, etc.

wholestep, wholetone. An interval, such as C to D, equal to two halfsteps or semitones.

Index